Daily Inspiration from
LIVING RECOVERY

FREEDOM FROM FEAR

Fear is not a defect of character. If we were deprived of our capacity for fear we would be robots, not heroes. The goal of the Twelve Steps is not to destroy our human capacity for fear, but rather to transform our responses to fear and eventually change the nature of them.

HONESTY

Honesty was the beginning of recovery. We were finally able to ask for help. It was honesty with ourselves and others that broke through our denial and allowed us to admit we were powerless over alcohol or other drugs and that our lives had become unmanageable. It is an ongoing process.

FORGIVENESS

The task of forgiving ourselves seems monumental. But through the fellowship of love and caring, forgiveness is neither earned nor deserved—it is freely given. Forgiveness is for giving.

HOPE

Hope is a way of envisioning the future. It implies not only the wish that things will be different, but a willingness to change and the courage to act.

LIVING RECOVERY

Inspirational Moments for 12 Step Living

*by Men and Women
in Anonymous Programs*

A Hazelden Recovery Book
BALLANTINE BOOKS · NEW YORK

The contents of this book were originally published as twenty-two pamphlets in the Hazelden Pocket Power Series by the Hazelden Foundation in 1985, 1986, and 1987.

ISBN 0-345-36785-5

Manufactured in the United States of America

First Ballantine Books Edition: August 1990

Contents

Introduction

Moments. That's one way time is measured when you're recovering from an addiction. Days of moments, weeks of them, months, and finally years of moments. Each recovering moment becomes a brick in the foundation of a new life. Each one counts.

Life, of course, is a series of moments. Moments of despair, loneliness, and anger. Moments of great joy, tremendous faith, and peaceful serenity. No longer numbed by an active addiction, recovering people are bombarded with emotions wrenched from a painful past, a frightening present, and an uncertain, yet hopeful future. It is to the past, present, and future moments of recovering people that the authors of the enclosed chapters have written these brief inspirational messages. Whether you are in a recovery program yourself, or live or work with someone who is, *Living Recovery* offers insights and positive, helpful messages for understanding and living through life's ups and downs.

In the true spirit of the Twelfth Tradition of Alcoholics Anonymous—*Anonymity is the spiritual foundation of all our traditions, ever reminding us to place prin-*

ciples before personalities—the authors of this book
have all chosen to remain nameless. They are men and
women who wish to spread the message of their recovery program and to share what has worked for them in
their recovery from many different life problems, such
as alcoholism, drug, food, sex, and gambling addictions. They are also people whose lives have been
deeply affected by the addiction of a loved one; they
are codependents, parents, spouses, children, and coworkers of addicts.

If the terms *recovery* and *recovering* are words you
previously only associated with the recuperation from
physical illnesses, this use may, at first, seem awkward.
Some addictions, such as alcoholism or drug abuse, can
be more easily understood as a disease because the devastating physical effects of prolonged drinking or drug
use are evident. But addictions consume more than just
the physical health of a person. They also eat at the
emotional, intellectual, psychological, and spiritual
health. Recovering, then, means living a new life without the crutch of an active addiction and finding ways
to heal the damaged parts of our entire being. A "program of recovery" or being "in recovery" refers to
living the principles of a 12 Step program. There are
no "musts" in the program—not even within the principles. "The principles we have set down are guides to
progress. We claim spiritual progress rather than spiritual perfection," says the source of the 12 Steps, *Alcoholics Anonymous*.

Many of the words used to describe the absence of
an addictive substance or behavior are interchangeable.
Abstinent is the most common, encompassing term for
all addicts. Alcoholics are abstinent when they are sober—refraining from alcohol and other mood-altering
chemicals. For drug addicts, abstinence from mood-

altering chemicals (including alcohol) signifies they are "clean." Addictive gamblers are abstinent when they cease wagering. The definition for abstinence becomes more complex when the addictive substance is food, and yet there, too, those of us in Overeaters Anonymous refer to our abstinence—eating moderately while refraining from eating particular foods that trigger binge episodes. For the codependent and sex addict, the term refers to abstaining from compulsive, destructive behaviors.

Whether an obsession concerns a substance or a behavior, the addictive process is predictable and progressive. Without help, an addiction eventually leads to personal ruin and even death. With help, we can lead normal lives while we are forever mindful that we remain addicts. There can be no return to our addictive substance or behavior without once again becoming destructively engaged in our compulsion.

The term *enabling* defines the actions of those who love and are concerned about an addict. But, unlike its positive usage as described in dictionaries, enabling is a harmful assistance to active addicts because it helps their disease to continue. Giving money to, lying for, and cleaning up after addicts are ways in which we believe we are helping them, but in reality these actions only prolong addicts' activities.

Codependents are expert enablers. We know how (to the utmost of our time and energy) and when (all of the time) to provide assistance to others. This can become such a frenzied activity that we find our own needs are neglected. Codependents need to find balance in helping others *and* themselves.

Living Recovery is written with the wisdom only those who have been there can offer. These powerful, inspirational thoughts can help get you on track and keep you there as you follow your own program of recovery. Each reading offers insights and hope for dealing with the daily issues that you now face without food, drugs, sex, or codependency as an escape. And there are readings that serve as reminders of ways in which we can be grateful for our disease—grateful because we've found a way of living better than we ever had before.

"No wonder a moment's reflection on all we have to be grateful for does us so much good. It puts us squarely in the hands of our Higher Power." These are the words of the author of the chapter Gratitude. Again, in addition to reinforcing a strong program principle, we hear of the value of a moment's reflection—the purpose of this book. There are many themes woven throughout.

"Just for today I will be happy. It is my choice to be happy." That's the kind of keep-it-simple thinking used by many people in 12 Step programs to maintain quality recovery. It's not by accident that the simplest choice of words can succinctly define a very complex emotion or situation. "Just for today," a very popular reading by many 12-Steppers, supports the value of one-day-at-a-time abstinence. We need not worry about the past or the future. We commit to being sober, clean, abstinent for the twenty-four hours we are in. That's all. And perhaps we'll wake up tomorrow and make the same pledge—but we needn't worry about that today. Secondly, we are reminded that it is often our "choice" to be happy. What a revelation that can be—to discover that our happiness doesn't happen to us—it comes from within. Our happiness, or unhappiness, does not have to be an automatic reaction to a situation; Happiness is not the result of our wants and desires being fulfilled. It is, in many cases, how we *choose* to feel.

The positive, empathetic tone of each chapter is intended to bring about a change of attitude in the reader.

It is a supportive voice, such as a sponsor (a person with much experience in a 12 Step program) would offer a newcomer. It is a mini-meeting, if you will. Instant help during a rough moment when we find ourselves dealing with criticism, rejection, fear, inadequacy, or loneliness.

There are also chapters for reflection on such topics as prayer and meditation, miracles, serenity, and hope. We're often reminded of the Serenity Prayer: *God grant me serenity to accept the things I cannot change, courage to change the things I can, and wisdom to know the difference.*

Readings on the positive aspects of our recovery help us maintain an "attitude of gratitude" on such subjects as relationships, letting go, opportunities, and reaching out to others.

Throughout *Living Recovery*, the philosophy and the principles of the 12 Steps are supported through the various writers' interpretations. The original 12 Steps, which have been adapted for use by those with problems other than alcoholism, are as follows:

The Twelve Steps of Alcoholics Anonymous

1. We admitted we were powerless over alcohol—that our lives had become unmanageable.
2. Came to believe that a Power greater than ourselves could restore us to sanity.
3. Made a decision to turn our will and our lives over to the care of God *as we understood Him.*
4. Made a searching and fearless moral inventory of ourselves.
5. Admitted to God, to ourselves, and to another human being the exact nature of our wrongs.

6. Were entirely ready to have God remove all these defects of character.

7. Humbly asked Him to remove our shortcomings.

8. Made a list of all persons we had harmed, and became willing to make amends to them all.

9. Made direct amends to such people wherever possible, except when to do so would injure them or others.

10. Continued to take personal inventory and when we were wrong promptly admitted it.

11. Sought through prayer and meditation to improve our conscious contact with God *as we understood Him*, praying only for knowledge of His will for us and the power to carry that out.

12. Having had a spiritual awakening as the result of these steps, we tried to carry this message to alcoholics, and to practice these principles in all our affairs.*

A book like this one is not meant to be read in one sitting. Addictions usually grow and become destructive over long periods of time, and it is no wonder that building and maintaining strong recovery from them takes many bundles of single days. Thousands of recovering people have found that the words that follow provide the inspiration they need to "take one day at a time." Read ahead to find out why.

*From Alcoholics Anonymous, 3rd edition, © 1976, pp 59–60. Reprinted with permission.

JUST
FOR
TODAY

JUST FOR TODAY I WILL LIVE ONLY THESE PRE-cious 24 hours, I will focus on now. I needn't contem-plate the entire tapestry of my life, I need only consider how I shall weave the pattern of today with the thread of minutes and hours that is mine.

I will cherish the day as if it were my last. Today is yesterday's much-anticipated ''some day''—tomorrow's longed-for ''back when.'' I will hug this treasure of today to my chest, and regard the wonder of it with the same joy I behold a newborn. This day is new, and so am I.

Today I will not relive the past. I may look back, but I will not stare. I cannot live yesteryear's glories, nor can I erase yesterday's mistakes. In retrospect, I see how each event, joyful or sad, has led me to becoming who I am today. I will view my life as a journey, and gain perspective. I will not regret the past, but learn from it.

Today I will not agonize or worry about the future. Worrying is a waste of time. How many people, long since gone, worried that the Civil War would come? It came anyway. How many people have abandoned their businesses and homes to stand on a hill awaiting the end of the world? It hasn't happened yet. Tomorrow comes, for good or bad, despite the time I squander in anticipation. I will plan for tomorrow, live for today.

If my waking hours are spent recalling the past or anticipating the future, I am throwing away life's most precious gift: today. As such, I am throwing away life itself. For these 24 hours, I will give the day its due; I will start over tomorrow.

Today is my opportunity to start afresh. I am not responsible for yesterday or tomorrow. I am only responsible for today, and how I choose to live it. I will be here now.

JUST FOR TODAY I will be happy. It is my choice to be happy. I know that my attitude determines my state of mind. With a positive attitude and an open mind, I insure that I will retain my serenity no matter the circumstances of the day.

I am responsible for my happiness. I am not a puppet, controlled by the whims and moods of others. I have no control over others. I *do* control how I choose to react. I am not a button to be pushed by irritating coworkers, willful children, or honking strangers. I am like a deep, peaceful pool, unaffected by the winds which blow across my surface. My peace and my happiness come from within, and cannot be taken from me.

Others may act in a hurtful or irritating manner. I do not have to take it personally. I realize that another person's behavior toward me may say far more about them than it does me. If I am doing the right thing, I need not accept pain, anger, frustration, or blame. Nor will I blame others. I will remember that few people are evil; they may act as they do because they are insecure and ignorant—and neither circumstance warrants my becoming upset. I will give others the benefit of the doubt.

If pain is constant in my life, it indicates a need for me to change. Just as I would seek help in treating physical pain, I must resolve unhealthy attitudes and situations. I may treat it with prayer, talk with a trusted friend, or seek professional help, but I will accept the truth that pain is optional.

Today I will foster happiness in myself and others with a ready smile, gentle manner, sunny outlook, and confidence that happiness is God's plan for all people.

JUST FOR TODAY I will accept whatever is; I will not manipulate people and circumstances to suit my desires. I will let go and let God.

I will accept the premise that things happen for a reason. A circumstance may arise that I did not plan on or even desire. I will accept it as an opportunity. Instead of fighting the situation, I will look for the lesson to be learned. Instead of crying, Why me? I will ask, What can I learn from this?

As I leave behind my old behavior of trying to control everything and everyone, I will delight in the discovery that letting go and letting God brings prompter and more positive results than I ever dreamed. I will even learn to welcome the unexpected situation, as I search eagerly for the lessons which will help me grow to become wiser, more capable, and understanding.

Acceptance often entails forgiveness. I cannot deal with reality if I am continuing to nurture hurt, regret, or anger. I cannot move forward dragging this old baggage. The question is not, Do my enemies—those who have hurt me—deserve my love, but, Do *I* deserve my love? I will act in my own best interest by forgiving and accepting others. The past cannot hold me if I do not hold it.

Perhaps those who pass through my life are not friends or enemies, loved ones or strangers, as much as they are my teachers, each bringing a lesson, an example. Is there a trait I can emulate, one I should avoid? What does my reaction to this person—or that group—say about me? As I accept other people as they are, so I will gently accept myself, knowing that I am trying to become the person I was meant to be.

As I learn to let go and let God, I know inner peace. Peace and harmony pervade all my relationships. I am prosperous and my life is successful.

JUST FOR TODAY I will stretch my mind. I will consider a new idea, tackle a fresh topic, rethink a long-held opinion. I will learn something.

I recall the excitement of the first day of school, the anticipation as a child awakening to a long summer day. Do I have that sense of curiosity, that joy in learning, that delight in living? Have I allowed myself to grow bored and narrow in my thinking and my interests? If I am not constantly mentally growing and stretching, then I am not truly alive. Learning keeps me excited, anticipatory, stimulated, interested—and young in attitude. Old people who seem young are still learning.

As an adult, I do not have to learn in order to pass a test or earn a grade. Now I can learn for my own satisfaction, not to please a parent or impress a teacher. Nor need I undertake a broad, intellectual endeavor. Learning may be as simple as picking up an unknown magazine at the newsstand, going to a foreign film, eating at an ethnic restaurant, visiting a museum or art gallery, or attending a concert.

Now is the time for me to renew abandoned interests and to develop new ones. I may recover an old enthusiasm as I dig out the paints from the back of the closet, take my dusty collection from the attic. Inexpensive classes enable me to finally learn to swim, decorate cakes, snap better pictures, or speak a new language in time for my next vacation. I can join a bowling team, take up skiing, master the rules of football, take out a library card, or drift through the sky in a hot air balloon.

Today I will stop saying, "Someday I'll . . ." and dare to make my dreams and fantasies come true. Boredom and dull routine have no place in my life as I stretch and grow toward my potential of being an interesting person to others and to myself.

JUST FOR TODAY I will exercise my soul, growing emotionally and spiritually. I will learn the truth of the saying "It is more blessed to give than to receive" by extending myself to help another person without expecting thanks or even credit.

As I step outside myself to help another, I leave my own problems behind for a time and gain perspective on them. How often, in advising another, do I remind myself of wisdom I have forgotten to practice? Listening with care and concern to the problems of others expands my knowledge of the world and my understanding of human nature. Time sincerely invested in another person is seldom wasted.

I will grow emotionally as I learn to identify my feelings and to voice them before resentment and anger have the chance to build. I cannot expect even those who know and love me best to read my mind; I must take responsibility for my own emotional health by understanding myself so that I may help others to know me. Honesty with myself is essential if I am to be honest with others.

I can grow, too, by becoming more flexible, more spontaneous. Instead of meeting an idea or suggestion with why? I will ask myself, Why not? I will embrace life, not reject it. I will be as generous with myself as I am with others. I will be a yea-sayer, not a nay-sayer. I will not stew about small things. Asking myself, Will it matter in 50 years? is a way I can keep my life in perspective and inject a little humor into daily living, too. Today I will keep my emotions from leading me astray by asking myself, Is this the right thing to do? I am unerringly guided by that small voice within, which as a child, I knew as my conscience. Now I recognize it as a Higher Power which directs me toward good. When my emotions rage, I will sit quietly and listen for the guidance that is sure to come. There are no short-cuts to happiness. By doing the right thing in every circumstance I know the peace and emotional stability I long for. By doing the right thing I pay my dues to life; I pay my rent for space on this lovely earth.

JUST FOR TODAY I will be agreeable; I will reflect the expression and attitude I seek in others. I will not find fault or complain.

If I must correct children, students, or coworkers, I will do it kindly and in private, first pointing out what they are doing right before I call their attention to what should be corrected. If I am simply finding fault with another, I will look to myself first, remembering that when I point one finger of blame, three more point right back at me.

I will remember to smile. It will make me feel as good as the person who receives it. Anyone I may approach today will be more receptive to my requests and ideas if I present a pleasant, nonthreatening face to the world. My smile and friendly greeting may be the pick-me-up someone needed today. A smile won't break my face, and it may help heal another's broken spirit.

I will be as courteous to my family as I am to strangers. If charity begins at home, then so must the kindness, understanding, good will and encouragement that builds another's spirit and confidence. Those who love me deserve my best, not my least.

I will try to look my best. I needn't look like a movie star in order to make the most of nature's gifts. The picture I choose to present to the world illustrates what I think of myself, and may be my only opportunity to indicate that I am a person worth knowing.

Instead of searching for the right person, I focus on *becoming* the right person. Today I rate an *A* as I make an effort to be agreeable, approachable, and attractive.

JUST FOR TODAY I will be organized. I will set goals and make a plan for myself, so that when the day is done I can be satisfied with what I have accomplished.

By becoming more organized, I eliminate much of the clutter and chaos from my life. I will keep it simple at home and work by discarding items I do not use and by eliminating unproductive tasks. I will set in order the tools of work and leisure. I remember that disorganization is often a form of rebellion—like a teenager's messy room—but I am the one who suffers from the confusion in my life. If becoming organized seems an impossible task, I will borrow or buy one of the many books on the subject.

I will set for myself goals both simple and demanding, ranging from trying to smile more to taking a step toward achieving a long-cherished dream. I will write out my goals so that I may maintain my focus and feel the warm flush of success as I check off each accomplishment. I will not waste energy by talking of my goals. I will act. I know that all great achievements begin with small steps. Today I will begin my journey.

I will find it easier to accomplish my goals and avoid procrastination if I listen to that insistent voice within which directs my dreams and desires. Childhood's conscience is adulthood's Higher Power speaking. The voice is not my enemy, trying to pull me away from pleasure. It is my friend, nudging me toward my goals. I know my hopes and dreams are direction-pointers from God. I do not dream of the impossible.

Organization, and honesty, will help me be responsible. Honesty and responsibility equal integrity. I gain by becoming organized and setting goals.

JUST FOR TODAY I will enjoy a period of solitude to replenish my soul and insure serenity as a 24-hour state of mind.

As I work to become all that I can be, to accomplish all that I am capable of, I will remember that quiet contemplation is necessary to recharge my spiritual, emotional, and mental batteries. Time spent alone provides me with a perspective on my life that I cannot see when I am busy with daily demands.

I will not rush from activity to activity. I will allow the experience, the import, the enjoyment of each moment to soak in. How often have I longed for the days when time seemed to move more slowly? I know that I cannot slow down the world, but I can slow down my experience of it. I will leave myself ample time between activities so that I do not rush. During busy times, I will remember to breathe deeply, knowing that as I do so I inhale the energy of the universe and I am refreshed.

As I go through my day, I will stop to examine whether I am being efficient or frenetic. If I feel compelled to be constantly busy or in the company of others, perhaps I am avoiding quiet time alone because I do not wish to face myself. It is in solitude that I can best learn who I am. In stillness I can hear God voicing the direction in which I should go.

I needn't feel guilty or defensive over how I seek my solitude. I will take at last a half-hour each day for myself to be quiet and alone, whether it is closing my eyes as I ride the bus, enjoying summer clouds, bowing my head in church, or sitting in formal meditation on the floor of my room.

A regular period of solitude and application of the serenity prayer go hand-in-hand to insure a peaceful state of mind.

JUST FOR TODAY I will be unafraid. I will remember the words of Madame Curie: ''Nothing in life is to be feared, it is only to be understood.''

I know that ''for all things there is a season'' and for all things there is a reason. Whether I like the circumstances in which I find myself, I have confidence that there is a purpose, even if it is not immediately evident to me. I don't have to be afraid in any circumstance; I have only to look for the lesson I must learn.

How many times have I lost an opportunity because I was afraid of something new, of testing myself, of failing? I know that opportunity is God's invitation for me to grow and excel. When opportunity knocks, I must get up and answer; action is the key to my success. As I look back at opportunities I have let slip through my fingers—or even those at which I made a halfhearted attempt—I see that I lost out not because I am stupid or unworthy, but because I was afraid. Knowing my Higher Power is presenting me with a chance to grow, to realize my dreams, I need never fear opportunity again.

I am not afraid of life's challenges when I am prepared for them. I can prepare in several ways: by taking a small step each day toward realizing a dream, putting myself in another's place and speculating on what I would do, trying to do the right thing in every situation in my own life, and meditating or praying regularly to keep in tune with my Higher Power.

The next time I feel afraid—whether of making a speech or being involved with others in a potentially awkward situation—I will look to my Higher Power. I will say, "Thank you for the right words at the right time. Thank you for giving me the words and the actions to help others." With such gratitude in my heart, I am assured I will do and say the right thing at the right time.

If I always try to do the right thing, I have no reason to be afraid. I put my hand in God's, **JUST FOR TODAY**, and all is well.

Editor's Note:

This pamphlet is an elaboration of the principles brought forth in the popular message, "Just For Today," read by many people in Twelve Step programs.

HONESTY

A Story

Once some people heard of a place called the Cave of Truth. They discussed this among themselves and made further inquiries. Finally, they decided to set out in search of the cave and after a long and difficult journey, they found it. At the entrance sat an old man who was the guardian. They approached him and asked if indeed this was the Cave of Truth. He assured them that it was. They asked if they might enter. In reply he asked, "How deeply into the Cave of Truth do you want to go?" At this question, they retreated and talked among themselves. They returned and said, "We would like to enter and go just deep enough to say we have been there."

This story may remind us of our reaction when we are told to grasp and develop a manner of living which demands rigorous honesty. We may discover a part of us wants to be honest just enough to claim we have been there. Ongoing recovery, however, demands that we do more than simply visit truth and honesty as though they were a part of a scenic tour. The program tells us we have to go deeply into the Cave of Truth by growing in honesty or run the risk of relapse. As some people say, "Either grow or go."

For many of us, honesty was the beginning of recovery. We were finally able to ask for help. It was honesty with ourselves and others that broke through our denial and allowed us to admit we were powerless over alcohol, other drugs, food, or sex and that our lives had become unmanageable. Many of us struggled with that First Step, sometimes for years.

We may have been plagued by doubts surrounding a phrase in Chapter Five of the A.A. Big Book which says those people who do not recover cannot or will not completely give themselves to this simple program, usually people who are constitutionally incapable of being honest with themselves. Such doubts about our capacity to be rigorously honest may be with us well into recovery. We discover that honesty is indeed an ongoing process and our tendencies to be dishonest, even in little things, can be a source of discouragement.

However, when we remember that honesty was the key to the beginning of our recovery, we can understand how important honesty is for our growth in all that recovery and life have to offer. The Twelve Step program is designed to help us grasp and develop this manner of living.

Blocks to Honesty

Why do we find it difficult to be honest even when we want to be? Perhaps one reason is that dishonesty had become for us a way of life when we were trapped in our addiction. Dishonesty permeated our behavior as well as our minds and emotions. Frequently we lived in a world of illusions that we could scarcely discern from the world of reality. We found ourselves telling lies even when the truth was more convenient.

We developed a lifestyle around our addictions and compulsions that demanded we be dishonest. We would lie concerning our whereabouts, about the money we were spending on drugs or food or gambling, and about how important drinking was to us. We became emotionally dishonest to the point that we did not know what our real feelings were because our emotions were under the sway of our addictions and compulsions.

Dishonesty had become such a way of life that it will take time and effort to change. We are sometimes tempted in recovery to think we have gotten "totally honest." The Twelve Step program suggests that absolute honesty is impossible. Rather, we have the capacity to grow in honesty. To do this, we need to make the effort ourselves, but we also need to be with people who are becoming honest, too. As we experience their honesty, whether with themselves in relation to their Higher Power or in relation to us, we discover our capacity for honesty grows and develops.

Another significant block to honesty is fear. There is a risk involved in honesty, and frequently we fear the consequences and pain that it may cause. It is helpful if we can be honest about our self-centered fear and share that with others. They may help us see that the consequences of our dishonesty in a given situation are more painful and dangerous for us than being honest.

Honesty and the Steps

There are times when we think, "I have worked the Steps. I have done a Fourth and a Fifth Step once and I don't need to do them again." That may, in fact, be true for many of us. However, some find it helpful to do these Steps over again after some length of recovery. Others make it a regular practice to do a Tenth Step, not only on a daily basis, but on a semiannual or annual basis as well. The inventory Steps can help us grow in honesty. These Steps, particularly later in recovery, can reveal patterns of denying our good qualities, patterns in which we tend to avoid opportunities for growth.

At first, honesty regarding ourselves tends to focus on the negative dimensions of our behavior and personality. This honesty about ourselves, particularly as we share it with others, begins to free us from the self-deception we have engaged in because of our addiction compulsion. Perhaps it is more difficult for us to be honest about our good qualities and the basic goodness of our personalities.

Many of us were mental and emotional wrecks and spiritually bankrupt when we began the program. Honesty serves first to clear the ground regarding our past and present condition. But as we grow in recovery and personal awareness, we become conscious of other more positive dimensions of our lives that the disease kept hidden. Sometimes we are even fearful of acknowledging our good qualities. It may seem like grandiosity, or we may fear the responsibility that comes with this recognition. But this personal awareness of our talents and abilities can open new vistas of growth. We discover, for example, our lives have purpose and meaning; we can be useful to others, and we have something to contribute to life Frequently it takes as much courage to be honest about our goodness as it does about the negative dimensions.

The Twelve Steps continually encourage us to be honest with ourselves by being honest about ourselves with others. Through the Eighth and Ninth Steps we are led into a new quality of honesty with other people. These Steps suggest that we examine our past and acknowledge the harm we may have caused others. The ''Big Book'' devotes a number of pages to these important Steps. One point that seems to emerge is the importance of discussing our amends with someone we trust before we make them. Making amends is different than making an apology. Many of us are experts at saying, ''I'm sorry.'' However, an amend implies a willingness to change our behavior toward another person. We are not only saying, ''I'm sorry,'' we are saying, ''I intend not to treat you that way in the future.'' Honesty in these Steps may also mean we need to repay, as best we can, someone we harmed financially or emotionally. Step Nine tells us we are to do this except when it would injure the person we are making amends to or others.

To do the Eighth and Ninth Steps honestly, we need to examine our motives and intentions in a detailed way. In early recovery we may have thought we were making amends when all we were really trying to do was get our own way, or get someone out of our hair, or bring about reconciliation. To work these Steps honestly is to acknowledge the harm we have done to others in an honest and forthright manner and to be willing to accept the consequences of our actions. Sometimes a nagging discontent in recovery is due to our unwillingness to really make amends to people whom we may have harmed. The Big Book clearly suggests that we need help on these Steps in special ways. The Big Book reminds us that we are experts at hiding dubious motives beneath good reasons, and sharing with others can help us avoid this. Discussing amends with people in the program can help us discover when we need to make amends and how we can best do this.

What is Honesty, How Does it Flourish?

One way of defining honesty is to say it is simply the lack of intention to deceive. When we intend not to deceive ourselves, others, and God as we understand Him, we are making solid progress in developing that manner of living which requires rigorous honesty. We discover we can go deep into the Cave of Truth and become more free and at ease. We lose our fear of being honest with others and of their being honest with us. We find the consequences of being honest are better than continuing dishonesty. Developing honesty may at times be difficult and hard work. It may require time and trust in others to discover what honesty is for us in a given situation or at a particular time in our lives. But as we grow in honesty, we will appreciate its benefits.

We need to be careful about being brutally honest. When we, or someone around us, is being brutally honest, chances are we are being more brutal than honest. Honesty flourishes in an atmosphere of care. For people in recovery, honesty is nourished by the care we have for one another as fellow sufferers from the same addiction and compulsive behavior. Without care, honesty becomes false.

Another quality surrounding honesty is patience. Many of us have been dishonest for a long time, and it will take a while for us to develop an honest way of living. We tend at times to fall back into old patterns of behavior. Our honesty and the honesty of others in the program can help us avoid these patterns. When we attempt to develop honesty and other qualities, we need to be aware of the principle of *progress not perfection*. Honesty is the work of a lifetime. We need to acknowledge the progress that has been made, but at the same time we acknowledge the distance from our goal. Having patience with ourselves and with others can help us develop an honest quality of life.

Perhaps another story will illustrate how honesty flourishes. Michelangelo was a great sculptor. Every day a small boy would come by his studio and watch. One day after the boy had been watching Michelangelo work for months on a particular piece of marble, the child asked, "What is it that you are really doing?" Michelangelo looked at him and said, "There is an angel in this stone and I am trying to let him out." His work demanded care and patience, and so does honesty. As we strive to become more honest, we discover that we need care and patience, too. We may not be trying to free angels from stone, but we are trying to discover and free our selves.

Sometimes it may seem that honesty is a dangerous thing. At a meeting on the topic of honesty someone said, "What would happen if the whole world suddenly became honest?" The reaction of many was that it would be a disaster, a total catastrophe. They assumed the dishonesties of the world are what keep it going. Before this mood could catch on, a young woman said, "Perhaps if the world were suddenly honest, the sheer beauty would overwhelm us all." It is not the dishonesties in the world and in our lives that keep them going. In fact, dishonesties make life harder. Honesty, the willingness to live with the intention of not deceiving ourselves, others, and God as we understand Him, enables us to be the people we truly are.

Help in Being Honest

One way of viewing the illness of chemical dependence or other forms of compulsive behavior is to look at what is hidden by it and through it. Certainly we hid our addiction from friends, family, and even from ourselves as best we could. As our illness progressed it began to hide other things. We covered up many dimensions of our lives as well. The process of getting better can be understood as uncovering, recovering, and discovering accomplished through honesty.

We need to do more than simply uncover the truth about our powerlessness over our addictions and compulsions. We need to uncover the truth about ourselves as human beings. This demands a willingness to look at aspects of our lives which we may want to hide from others. This continuing willingness to uncover the truth is a necessary step before we can move further in recovering.

As we go more deeply into the Cave of Truth and are more willing to uncover things that in the past we feared looking at, our process of recovery continues. We begin to discover new and glorious things about ourselves and others that we never knew before. This discovery can be an exciting and adventurous time of growth. We may discover talents we did not know we had; we may discover we are willing to take new risks in our growth that amaze us; we discover we have something to offer other people.

Again, honesty is the key to discovery. Many times we need others to help us discover these new dimensions of our personalities. When we can accept their honest evaluation of us, we are in the real process of self-acceptance and growth. Step Ten continues the uncovering process by taking a personal inventory and admitting when we are wrong. This Step presupposes that we will be wrong for it says *when*, not *if*. This reminds us that we aim at making progress and have not become perfect. It also enables us to guard against old behaviors and attitudes coming back into our lives. We continue the process of uncovering, recovering, and discovering by taking note of motives, intentions, and actions toward others and ourselves.

If honesty is the lack of intention to deceive, a daily Tenth Step may reveal that there are many ways in which we can, and often do, deceive ourselves and those around us. Sometimes it may be in words, other times it may be in gestures or actions. The willingness to look at this on a daily basis can be a freeing experience. And a Tenth Step based on honesty can make a significant difference between a mediocre and somewhat uncomfortable recovery and one that is deep, joyous, and fulfilling.

We may find taking a Tenth Step not only on a daily basis but on a quarterly or semiannual basis is also helpful. This gives us an opportunity to look at our lives and see what patterns we need to be aware of. The willingness to share a written Tenth Step with a trusted friend, spiritual advisor, or sponsor can be a tremendous tool in our growth. Many of us have found that we cannot be honest with ourselves unless we are honest with another person. This does not mean that we have to call someone every day and tell them of our dishonesties. But the willingness to share with someone what is going on with us is a certain aid in our growth and honesty.

Many people have found doing a Tenth Step in the form of a journal can be a helpful experience in recovery. For example, we could record not only the dishonesties of the day, but also those things we have to be grateful for. We can go into detail about our hopes, dreams, fears, and the relationships in our lives.

There are many books available on keeping a journal. What we need to remember most of all is that this is our private journal, to be shared only when we wish. It is a place where we can be honest with ourselves, and an opportunity to explore what is important for us. We can write in our journals as though no one else would ever see it, even though we may choose to share it with someone later. Most of us know ourselves well enough to recognize that if we are writing with the possibility of someone reading it, we will write more for them than for ourselves.

Honesty seems to be one of the central qualities of continuing recovery. As the Big Book says, we are attempting to grasp and develop a manner of living that demands rigorous honesty. This does not always need to be a frightening process. Pain may be involved, but there is also freedom, joy, and fulfillment as we are able to grow in honesty with ourselves, others, and our Higher Power. Should someone ask us why we are making such an effort at honesty, we can reply as Michelangelo did. "There is an angel in this stone and I am trying to let him (or her) out."

GREAT
EXPECTATIONS

You MAY REMEMBER BEING ON A "PINK CLOUD" shortly after you began your recovery. As the fog caused by your addiction or compulsion lifted, you began to feel good for the first time in months or even years. You felt so good, in fact, you were sure your problems were over forever. Undoubtedly, your sponsor warned you the euphoria wouldn't last. But if you were like most of us, you secretly expected it would. And sure enough, our sponsors were right.

Eventually, we fall off our cloud and begin to deal with life as it really is, rather than as we wish it to be. Through intensive work on the Steps, we begin to understand our lives on a spiritual plane. We achieve some serenity, the promises begin to come true, and we're on our way to a lasting recovery.

Why Expectations Can Be a Problem

When we've been abstinent for a few years, we're likely to run into some problems we didn't expect. We've learned, for the most part, the meaning of "one day at a time." We probably aren't going to a meeting every night like we did in the beginning. Our jobs are working reasonably well; our relationships with others have smoothed out a bit. In short, the program is working both for us and in us. We're beginning to understand serenity and know some real peace of mind. Life is looking pretty good.

Problems begin when we expect the good life will be ours forever, without a hitch. We get into trouble when we count on a particular person, place, or situation to bring us exactly the results we want when we want it, or when we make unreasonable demands on ourselves. Life just doesn't flow smoothly, and if we expect it to, we're setting ourselves up for disappointment or worse.

Not all expectations, of course, lead to difficulties. After all, "to expect" simply means to look forward to something or to anticipate something. It's when our expectations grow out of proportion that problems develop. Our addictive personalities seem to make it easy for us to create grandiose visions as we anticipate the results of almost any action. This wouldn't be so bad if we didn't insist our expectations be met. But instead of responding to our unfulfilled expectations reasonably, we tend to react as if the world has ended.

Disappointment, that feeling of being totally let down, gets us into the most trouble. When our expectations are not met, we begin to feel isolated and alone. We wonder what's wrong with us, with our world, and with God. Carried to the extreme, these feelings can lead to a slip because they create the sense there's no point in going on.

Three Kinds of Expectations

It's possible to classify expectations in three ways: the expectations we place on ourselves, those we place on others, and those we place on things and situations. Any of these can be destructive, and often they work together.

We usually find we are expecting a great deal from ourselves—perhaps more than we would expect from anyone else. And when we fail to live up to these self-imposed expectations, we're harder on ourselves than anyone else would be.

What's happening here? Why do we place such demands on ourselves, then beat ourselves up when we think we fail? It's partly because we've enjoyed a little success in recovery, and we want more. We haven't yet learned our limits or how to bring balance to the goals we set for ourselves. It's also partly because we feel we must find a way to make up for the time we lost while we were practicing addicts. We think we have to rush madly about to achieve the success that surely would have been ours if we hadn't been addicted.

Take, for example, the woman who almost came apart because she didn't receive an expected promotion. At a meeting, her story went something like this: "I'm just not good enough. No matter how hard I try I can never measure up. I don't know what's the matter with me."

This is not a balanced response. Obviously, the woman had expectations far beyond the reality of the situation. Chances are she had engaged in fantasies about what it would be like to have the extra money and the additional prestige. It's quite possible, too, that she did nothing but fantasize. We can get so caught up in our expectations that we fail to take necessary actions.

But this person could have avoided the problem in the first place by not getting tangled up in expectations. From the program point of view, the problem here is the emotional upset, not the failure to get the promotion.

We also tend to expect a lot from the people around us. If we're parents, we expect more from our kids. We expect more from our coworkers, spouses, and friends. In fact, it's possible to demand so much from others that we put a heavy strain on our relationships.

A classic example of this happens at least once to all of us when we're doing Twelve Step work. A newcomer expresses the desire to have what we have, and we immediately lay plans to help them get, and stay, abstinent. We plan what meetings they should go to and when they should work their Fourth Step. Underlying our intentions is the demand that they get abstinent our way, and if they don't, we're crushed.

If the woman who didn't get promoted had blamed other people, she might have sounded like this at a meeting: "I don't understand it! I have seniority. The person they promoted doesn't know half as much as I do. It's not fair. I'll show them, I'll quit—better yet, I'll sue." In this instance, she is failing to take any responsibility herself and totally blaming other people. Again, the root cause is expectations.

The third type of expectation we often have to deal with is the expectation we hold for places and things. How many people have you known who have taken a vacation and come home disappointed? Or what about the person who is disappointed with a new car or other purchase? When this happens we are looking outside ourselves for a quick fix. We think the new clothes or new apartment are the keys to happiness. Although there is certainly nothing wrong with material possessions, they will not give us contentment—and to expect them to is a sure way to be disappointed.

How do we let these expectations of ourselves and others sneak up on us? Perhaps it's just another example of the pendulum swinging too far. When we came to the program we were whipped, sure we were condemned to a boring life made up of nothing but meetings and the constant struggle to stay abstinent. With time, we discovered our lives could be fuller and more productive than we had ever dreamed possible. So we swung to the opposite extreme, expecting serenity, fame, fortune, and love. We placed high demands on ourselves and others.

Some Solutions

So what are we to do? We've worked the Steps, we've gone to lots of meetings, we've been involved in service, and all of a sudden the bottom drops out of our world. What now?

The first step is to recognize the problem. It's probably safe to say that any time you feel any disappointment at all, it's because you've had expectations that haven't been met. Usually there's some sort of warning. Often it's easy to ignore the first signals. We may find ourselves discounting little disappointments that crop up, only to discover they are happening with greater frequency. If we don't catch the symptoms quickly, we're likely to find ourselves either worn down by a whole series of little disappointments, or suddenly faced with a truly large one.

The quickest way to deal with any disappointment is to do a spot-check inventory when it happens. This can be simply a matter of asking, "Why am I disappointed? What did I expect to happen in this situation?" When we answer these questions honestly, we're apt to see we were placing unreasonable demands on ourselves, someone else, or the situation. Once we get a handle on the demand we've made, we can let it go immediately.

It's also helpful to ask, "What can I learn from this?" Of course, one thing is not to have our expectations so high. But we can look a bit deeper and see if we wanted a certain outcome simply to enhance our own view of ourselves or for some other entirely selfish reason.

It's generally true that when we want something only for ourselves, without understanding the contribution we can make to others, we end up disappointed. So checking for selfishness and self-centeredness is also helpful.

Sometimes we need to do a more thorough overhaul of our attitudes. Again, an inventory, this time perhaps a written one, is a good way to start. By writing down several recent disappointments, our response or reaction to them, and asking the same sorts of questions, we're likely to discover a pattern. We may discover we are simply being selfish, or we are trying to run the show our way, or we've been expecting something for nothing.

It's easy to get confused about the difference between planning and projecting—projecting is just another term for expectations. There is nothing wrong, of course, with making plans. In fact, if we didn't make plans nothing much would get done. The problems arise when we demand our plans turn out the way we expect them to. We must learn not to demand or count on specific results.

Life is a Series of Adjustments

One way of looking at life is to see it as a constant series of adjustments. It's not unlike driving down a road; in order to get to the store, you don't simply point your car in that direction—you follow the road, which is probably not a direct line from your house to the shopping center. And in order to stay on the road, you must make constant adjustments with the steering wheel and the gas pedal.

If you held the wheel in one position, you'd find yourself in the ditch. Expecting a specific result is rather like holding the steering wheel in one position. It's difficult to be flexible and to respond when we take the bit in our teeth, determined we're going to achieve our outcome no matter what.

When we're driving, we get to our destination not only by having a goal, but by making constant adjustments using feedback. We may notice, for instance, that we're headed a bit too far to the right, so we turn the wheel to the left. Perhaps we then notice we've overcompensated and are moving too close to the center, so we turn the wheel a bit to the right. We do this almost unconsciously, and, after making hundreds of these corrections we find ourselves safely at the store.

The same thing is true of life; if you want to be president of the company, you make plans based on your understanding of what it takes to be president. Perhaps you discover along the way that you need an extra course in business administration, so you make that adjustment. That doesn't mean your plans were wrong, just that you didn't have all the information.

The more flexible our plans are, the more likely we'll get where we want to go. When we're caught up in expectations, we can get locked into a particular course of action that turns out to lead in a different direction. Then we're unhappy because our expectations were not met.

We also may find, along the way, that our plans change. For example, we may need to go to the store after a storm, but we discover the road is closed. We then either decide to go back home and make do with what we have, or head in another direction to another store. The same thing is true about wanting to be president—we may find we are not willing to take another course, so we change our goal. If the goal is a good relationship, it doesn't work to place our hopes and expectations on one person until we're sure they return the feeling. Even then, we must avoid expecting that person to be the key to our happiness.

There's another attitude some of us acquire as we continue on the road to recovery. We feel we've already done so much, and we've been so good that we deserve to have our expectations met just because we're wonderful people. This is a particularly subtle notion, often showing up without our even realizing it.

Sometimes it takes the form of bargaining with God. We may actually be expecting God to provide us with some wonderful result, in spite of the fact we're not putting much effort into it. It's as if we were saying to ourselves, "Look, I've been abstinent five years now, things really ought to be going better." Well, perhaps they should and perhaps not. What we receive from life really depends on what we put into it.

We will also discover as we continue in recovery that

we tend to become involved in more things. Because we're getting well, we're able to take more risks. The more we do and the more risks we take, the more disappointments we will have if we don't learn how to temper our expectations with reality.

So our solution is to get back into the Steps again. First we need to concentrate on our inventory to discover where we went wrong. Then we need to continue to deepen our conscious contact with the God of our understanding through prayer and meditation. Finally, we need to reach out to others, perhaps in Twelve Step work, practicing the principles as we go along. It's a process of surrender.

Acceptance

Acceptance is the key. We must come to terms with ourselves and discover just what we are capable of doing, not what we wish we could do. We need to learn that, like ourselves, every other person is doing the best he or she can. We must recognize that true happiness and satisfaction come to us through our Higher Power and not by anything we do strictly on our own. We must come to terms with the fact that nothing happens to us without a purpose. Everything we do is an opportunity for growth, as long as we're willing to look at it that way.

Steps Ten, Eleven, and Twelve, the so-called maintenance Steps, can go a long way toward keeping our expectations at the delightful status of simply looking forward to tomorrow without the demand that it be to our order and on our terms.

PATIENCE

PATIENCE IS AN ELUSIVE GOAL FOR RECOVERING PEO-
ple, one we need to work at everyday. In our efforts to
become patient, we face many obstacles. Some of the
most formidable are self-centeredness and self-will, a
low tolerance for pain, lack of discipline, our rush to
gain lost time, and perfectionism.

These obstacles are familiar; they are some of our
old character defects, the symptoms of our disease. We
can overcome these obstacles if we are willing to devote
ourselves to a program of spiritual growth. While we
may never become truly patient people, it is possible,
in fact, it is essential, to keep from being driven by
impatience.

Freedom from the Bondage of Self

When we were using, we thought the world revolved
around us. At the center of the universe, we played the
maestro, trying to direct the orchestra of people and
events in our lives. When people didn't behave as we

wished, when circumstances didn't proceed according to our design, we became impatient and pressed harder to get control. When the full force of our will failed to bring the desired results, we became angry, resentful, and self-pitying. More often than not, those negative feelings provided us with a good excuse for using. That is what the Big Book calls "self-will run riot."

In taking the First Step on the road to recovery, we admitted we hadn't done such a great job of managing the show. Not only could we not control the world, but in the face of our addictions or compulsions, we were powerless over ourselves. When we saw people in the program who had begun to recover from their illness and rebuild their lives, we came to believe that by relying not on our own will, but on the help of a Higher Power, we, too, could regain some sanity in our lives. In time we were able to let go our choke hold on self-will, and made a decision to turn our will and our lives over to a God of our own choosing.

Through our experience in the program, we have learned that letting go and letting God is not a one-time choice that forever frees us from self-will. We need to make that decision over and over again, when we don't get the promotion we think we deserve, when a loved one doesn't return our affections, when our child misbehaves. Whenever things don't go our way, our self-will tempts us to take back control from our God. Such slips need not discourage us. We realize recovery is just a beginning; it does not result in an overnight change of character. Recovery is a process, and our character defects wear off gradually.

By practicing the principles of the Twelve Step program, we can daily reaffirm our decision to rely on God's will rather than our own. When we feel ourselves becoming impatient and willful, we can turn to our

Higher Power and ask for help in overcoming our self-will. This Third Step prayer can help: "God I offer myself to Thee—to build with and to do with me as Thou wilt. Relieve me of the bondage of self, that I may better do Thy will. Take away my difficulties, that victory over them may bear witness to those I would help of Thy Power, Thy Love, and Thy Way of Life. May I do Thy will always!"

When we pray, we can be secure in the knowledge that all of our prayers *are* answered. The answers may not be the ones we hoped for, and they might not come when we expect. God's answers come in their own special time, place, and manner. As we make progress in our recovery, we will find that our will becomes more and more like God's will for us. As that happens, our troubles with impatience diminish.

The Lessons of Pain

Patience comes from the Latin word meaning *to suffer*. When we began our recovery, we realized we had little experience in suffering. For years we had tried to avoid suffering, to dull the pain by using. For a time, it seemed to work. The booze (or pills, or food, or co-dependency, whatever the object of our addiction) numbed us against pain, and against the rest of our feelings, too. It is not surprising that, once we removed the buffer that separated us from the real world, we were overwhelmed by the hurt. We had not developed the patience to suffer through pain.

Through recovery, we are learning life is sometimes difficult, full of pain as well as joy. Now we see we cannot get around life's problems by ignoring them or by deadening ourselves against the pain so we can forget the problems that caused that pain.

Pain is a natural part of our growth and development as human beings. Benjamin Franklin said, "Those things that hurt, instruct." Our friends in the program remind us: "No pain, no gain." There are many lessons to be learned from pain, if only we have the willingness to learn them. If we but ask, God will give us the courage to stop running away from painful situations, to face pain head-on, and deal with it honestly.

One of the lessons of pain is that it motivates us to change. Change is difficult for all of us. We tend to cling to our old habits because they are familiar and safe. Even when an old behavior hurts us, we prefer it to the unknown risks of change. It is often only when the pain of our old ways overwhelms us that we will stop resisting change and the growth that it holds.

Another of the lessons of pain is gratitude. Our ability to feel pain signals the return of our other feelings, including joy, love, and serenity. As we learn to "stand still and hurt," we become thankful to God for reawakening our capacity to experience fully the range of human emotions.

When we are hurting, it is helpful to remember two things. First, nothing lasts forever. It is much easier to face the difficulties of the moment when we remind ourselves that this, too, shall pass. Second, God never burdens us with more than we can handle. If we had to face all the trials of a lifetime in one day, we would be devastated by the suffering. But we are not called upon to do that. If we concentrate on suffering through only today's trials and trust in God's Power to see us through them, we will grow in patience.

One Day at a Time

A Sanskrit proverb challenges us: "Look to this day, for it is life, the very life of life. In its brief course lie all the realities and verities of existence, the bliss of growth, the splendor of action, the glory of power—for yesterday is but a dream, and tomorrow is only a vision, but today, well-lived, makes every yesterday a dream of happiness and every tomorrow a vision of hope. Look well, therefore, to this day."

Why is it so hard for those suffering from addictions or compulsive behaviors to live one day at a time? One reason is that we want what we want *when we want it*. When we were using or acting out, our self-discipline was limited to doing what was needed to protect our supply. Our single goal was the immediate pleasure provided by a drink or a pill or a chocolate bar. Part of patience is recognizing the difference between our needs and our wants. It means trusting that our real needs will always be met.

Recovery helped us clear the cobwebs out of our minds. Recovery has enabled us to take an honest look at our lives and make some sane choices about the course we want to take. We see that in order to achieve our goals, we need to get some discipline in our lives and learn how to pass up the pleasure of immediate gratification in favor of long-term objectives.

It is hard to practice perseverance, to keep on hoeing the long row, especially when the end is out of sight. One of the keys to developing self-discipline is accepting responsibility for our lives. Turning our will and our lives over to God does not relieve us of accountability. We choose how we think and feel and act, and we choose the consequences of those thoughts, feelings, and actions. Understanding that will help us put forth our best efforts each day, knowing that God will give us the strength to face tomorrow.

Keeping it simple is good advice when we are building self-discipline. By starting out with small, reasonable goals, we maximize our chances of reaching them. Even one small success can do much to bolster our confidence and reinforce our efforts. Sharing our goals with someone in the program is another way to strengthen our resolve. It has the added benefit of gaining us the support and encouragement of a friend. By being responsible for those things we can affect and relying on our Higher Power for what is beyond our control, we can learn to welcome each day as a new beginning.

Slowing Down

Many people miss the magic of the present moment because they are dashing about, trying to accomplish too much too fast. For recovering people, "life in the fast lane" can lead to disaster. We may think we have good reason to rush. When we were in recovery, we noticed how limited our lives had been when we were chemically dependent or addicted to other forms of compulsive behavior. Our spiritual and emotional growth had been stunted by our illness. We were anxious about all the years we had "wasted." And we were impatient to make up for lost time, to hasten our development, and fill our empty lives. We threw ourselves into every experience we encountered, befriended everyone we met, turned our lives upside down in a massive self-improvement campaign.

In our compulsive activity, we may forget to tend to our basic spiritual, emotional, and physical needs. At meetings, people remind us "easy does it." They also point out to us the warning signals telling us to HALT: hungry, angry, lonely, tired. We need to pay attention to those warning signals, just as we must heed the warning lights on our dashboard.

Practicing the Eleventh Step will help us slow down. Prayer and meditation, moments of quiet communion with our Higher Power, calm our urgent need to move. They help us gain the perspective that we cannot see in the midst of our busyness. Slowing down is essential to balance, and balance nurtures patience.

Acceptance, Forgiveness, and Gratitude

Perfectionism is another hindrance to patience, for it robs us of gratitude. Perfectionism is the stubborn insistence that life must conform to our idealistic idea of what should be. We create a no-win situation for ourselves by setting standards so high that no one could possibly meet them. When, as inevitably happens, we fail to make the grade, we are filled with frustration, hopelessness, and self-loathing. Our unrealistic expectations blind us to the real headway we are making in recovery. This all-or-nothing attitude makes us impatient with others as well as with ourselves, for we find our coworkers, family, and friends are all imperfect human beings, too.

How do we combat such defeatist thinking and find a middle path between being absolutely perfect and perfectly worthless (that is, the path of being human)? To start, we summon all the honesty and humility we can muster, and we admit our mistakes. Taking a daily inventory will help us do that. But admitting our mistakes, in itself, is not enough to quiet our impatience. We must go a step further, and *forgive* ourselves for our human shortcomings. Forgiveness fosters self-love and acceptance, and makes possible acceptance and love of others and the world around us.

Acceptance shifts our focus from what is *not* to what *is*. Looking at life with clear eyes, unfogged by perfectionism, we cannot help but see how much we have to be grateful for. By daily renewing our appreciation of all of life—its ups and downs—we close the door on perfectionism and free ourselves from impatience.

SURRENDER

"SOME OF US HAVE TRIED TO HOLD ON TO OUR OLD ideas and the result was nil—until we let go absolutely," is from Chapter Five of the Big Book and is read daily at thousands of A.A. meetings.

The same idea is repeated in different ways at other Twelve Step recovery group meetings. The basic message is that we recover only by completely giving up attitudes and practices that create problems.

Surrender is what's needed to let go. It doesn't come easily for most of us. Many of us have difficulty accepting a recovery program, while others make half-hearted attempts to recover only to relapse later. And even those among us who achieve recovery and freedom from compulsive behavior have trouble surrendering bad habits and ideas which create problems in our new lives.

Resist it though we may, *surrender* is the only door to recovery. It is also the door to growth in recovery. Real surrender includes a powerful desire for change, as well as a complete readiness to part company with our old ways. It is a realization that change is necessary even though it includes risk and pain. People have stayed abstinent in Twelve Step programs for years; however, after having slips they've admitted they haven't really surrendered the old ideas that led to drinking.

Every Step of the A.A. or any other Twelve Step program includes surrender. The biggest hurdle, of course, is the First Step, which means surrendering our badly misplaced belief that we can handle our addiction or codependency. The Second and Third Steps call for surrender to a Higher Power. Along the way, there is also the Sixth Step, which takes up the matter of becoming "entirely ready" to surrender one's defects of character. All of the Twelve Steps can be difficult challenges for us and other compulsive, rebellious people.

Why is Total Surrender Necessary?

In dealing with other problems and shortcomings, we may try to avoid total surrender by hanging on to things which still seem important to us: a little gossip, a resentment now and then, hidden excursions into sex, a few dishonesties, etc. We are dismayed and bitter when such things backfire on us. We may even discover we have to make the same *total* surrender of other problems as we did when we gave up our addictive substance or behavior. The middle ground in anything can often be a bed of quicksand for the addict.

We hear proof of this problem in personal stories at meetings. Here are a few examples:

On Temper—
"Sure, I got into recovery. But I had an ugly temper that got even worse after I quit drinking, drugging, betting, etc. I made everybody pretty miserable with it. I

didn't want to live the program because a bad temper was useful to me, in a sick way. I could use it to put an end to an argument I was losing. I could blow my top and intimidate the kids. For a while, I even conned my wife into thinking it was her fault when I got mad. I finally started to deal with the problem when other people refused to take my s— any longer and I was forced to look at what I really was!''

On Resentments—

''Anybody who thinks you get over resentments just by staying abstinent is nuts. I had to get into recovery just to learn how *bad* my resentments were. I heard right away that you can release resentments by praying for the people who injured you and by wishing them well. I didn't really want to do that, and I kept on hurting. Finally it dawned on me that I secretly felt it was cowardly to forgive, and that if I had any real backbone I would try to get even. When I gave up this phony idea, I could also release my resentments, though it still comes hard.''

On Low Self-Esteem—

''I was embarrassed to learn that low self-esteem helped make me a show-off. Even before recovery, I hated myself for spending money on my addiction when the family was going without things they needed.

''I wish I could say my self-esteem improved dramatically when I started recovery. But there are times I still find myself saying and doing things simply to get approval or attention. I am still struggling with the strong belief that people won't like me if they really know me. And I have to learn that my real self—the person God created—is okay and doesn't need approval or attention.''

Barriers to Surrender

But even when one has been battered nearly to death, there may be formidable barriers in the path to surrender. The ego barrier, according to the late Dr. Harry M. Tiebout, is the most formidable block. A pioneer in the treatment of alcoholism, Tiebout insisted the inflated ego has to be surrendered before one can recover from alcoholism. He believed people under the sway of the inflated ego show three marked traits; namely, 1) the belief they are special or omnipotent; 2) an inability to accept frustration; and 3) an excessive drive with a need to do things quickly. With such people, selfish considerations always come first, and there is also an insensitivity to the needs and opinions of others. ''I want what I want when I want it,'' is the guiding motive.

We hear a lot about the inflated ego in recovery programs. It can make any of us squirm to review Tiebout's listing of the marked traits. In recovery, we can admit we thought we were ''special'' and that the ordinary rules and restrictions of society did not apply to us. We leaped into our addiction rather than accept frustration, and we often did things quickly (and perhaps sloppily) because our duties involved discomfort and boredom. We lived in a fantasy world and wanted to be relieved of the tasks and responsibilities others have to face. And even in recovery, the inflated ego can reassert itself and lead us into problems. A ''special'' person who didn't follow the rules once before can also become restive about the need to follow the Twelve Steps. A person who had trouble with frustration before may still struggle with it in recovery. And the need or drive to do things quickly always carries the possibility of trouble, because it can make us careless and inattentive. If there is any answer to these problems, it's probably in realizing the inflated ego and its traits always have to be surrendered anew.

Counterfeits of Surrender

Tiebout and other experts also identified false forms of surrender that lead both victims and their counselors astray. Perhaps one of the most deceptive counterfeits of surrender is *compliance*. It is especially deceptive because it can appear plausible and convincing.

People who find sanctuary in compliance fool themselves and others because they show outward signs of meeting the requirements for recovery. They will attend meetings, say the right things about their problem behaviors, will appear interested in the principles of recovery, and honestly seem grateful to be living a healthy life.

But the deadly shortcoming of compliance is that it takes place only on the surface. Compliance does not really touch the roots of the victim's problems. With compliance, thoughts and feelings that contributed to addiction remain intact, ready to break out with renewed bitterness. And by appearing to be so plausible and sincere, the complying person disarms those who might help penetrate the ego barrier. The victim neatly blocks any real examination of the thoughts and feelings that feed the insanity of addiction.

Yet the real problem with compliance is not that it deceives professionals and support group people who could otherwise be of help. The worst part of compliance is self-deception: the complying person may actually think he or she has really surrendered and that no further self-honesty is needed.

There is no foolproof way to tell whether another

person has truly surrendered or is only practicing compliance. But there may be a few clues which show how a person really feels. One clue is any tendency to blame our actions on people, places, or circumstances: "I can't stay sober as long as my wife insists on serving drinks at parties!" Or, "Who wouldn't want to gamble every night, living in a crummy town like this?" Or, "No wonder I developed a codependency, living with a man (woman) like that!" Another revealing clue is anything that shows overeating as a reward: "Getting my first college degree at age 35, I had a right to celebrate!" And compliance is usually evident when we tailor our behavior to the expectations of others but quickly revert to the old patterns when nobody is looking.

Compliance is not all bad, and it can serve a useful purpose by exposing the person to ideas and suggestions which may prove helpful later on, after true surrender occurs. However, the complying person is somewhat like the college student who attends classes but resists the learning process; the real message does not get through.

A second counterfeit of surrender is *submission*, which is similar to compliance. While drinking or overeating we tend to find protectors or strong people who will serve as enablers and help us continue our addictive behavior. In recovery programs, some addicts also seek out strong people who run their lives for them, sometimes without either party realizing what is happening. In submitting to another's direction, the person avoids real soul-searching and takes on, for a short time, the sponsor's attitudes and opinions. This means no real personal change is taking place. As with compliance, the person is merely making a surface change for the purpose of getting approval and acceptance.

Submission appears to work for a time, but it is likely

to end in rebellion, with both people bitter and disillusioned. The rebellious addict voices indignation and resentment over the way the sponsor has exercised dominance; while the sponsor, in turn, is bitter about the protégé's eventual rejection of the program: "I did everything for that guy but spoon-feed him, and he still relapsed on me!"

A third counterfeit of surrender could be termed the *blanket self-indictment*. This is a sweeping admission of total guilt and is usually accompanied by a statement such as: "When I came into the program, I was bankrupt in every respect—physically, financially, and morally." This statement is then used to imply that all problems, including character defects, have been surrendered and dealt with.

But this might be just a smoke screen to hide the really painful things that bother us. The blanket self-indictment is unsatisfactory because it does not focus on the *specific* problems and *exact* wrongs which cry for attention. We can actually be terribly sick in certain areas of our lives and still healthy in others, just as a person may have a weak heart and good lungs. It simply is not enough—and it is not true surrender—to say *everything* is wrong. We have to know just *where* and *why* we are hurting before we can really get well.

There may be other counterfeits of surrender. What we need to deal with, then, is the realization that only *true* surrender can carry the day for us—and it's our responsibility to let it happen. One surprising fact about surrender is that it takes place selectively, on the person's own time schedule. A person may have astonishing success in surrendering the substance of abuse, and yet fail repeatedly in surrendering another difficulty. We should not be too hard on ourselves when we fail. But we should not let ourselves off the hook by blaming our failure on mysterious forces rather than our own un-willingness to make a complete surrender.

Drawing Near to God: The Spiritual Surrender

Perhaps the highest hurdle in the recovery program is the idea of surrendering to a Higher Power, God as we understand Him. "Let Go and Let God," a slogan we often hear, is really a suggestion that we surrender our problems to a Higher Power and let this Power work in our behalf.

The strange thing about this phase of surrender is that most of us will admit it works for some people, and yet we may not be willing to let it work in our own lives. We know, for example, that people experience amazing and beneficial transformations as a result of religious conversions. This fact was a key point in advice the distinguished Carl Jung gave to a man in 1931—advice that led to the founding of Alcoholics Anonymous four years later. In the following years other Twelve Step groups (such as Gamblers Anonymous, Codependents Anonymous) were formed, based on A.A.'s Twelve Steps.

We might admire another person's spiritual experience or religious conversion, and yet be unable to accept the same ideas for our own lives. How can we pass over this barrier, which may be a very real one for us?

We can do it by striving for open-mindedness and a willingness to believe. A person can even stake out a position by accepting this statement as a sort of personal goal: "I know other people have been changed for the better by their belief in a Higher Power. I want the same experience for myself and for my own recovery. If it is possible for others, recovery is also possible for me. I am willing to surrender any preconceived ideas that might keep me from having a spiritual awakening, or what some call a spiritual rebirth. I am willing to listen to the experiences others share with me. I am willing to try prayer and meditation, or such other exercises that may help me in making contact with a Higher Power. And even if nothing happens for the time being, I will attend meetings of recovery groups and maintain an open mind about the possibilities of growth along spiritual lines.''

This is all that's needed or expected in the early phase. No person should be expected to make a real surrender to a Higher Power if he or she is not really convinced that it makes sense for them. Some of the early A.A.s, for example, asked people to pray with them on their knees, apparently in the belief that this induced the needed spiritual surrender. This practice was soon abandoned, probably because early members realized true surrender happens differently for each person.

Surrender to Win

Whatever it takes, surrender is the doorway to victory over all compulsions including alcohol and codependency. In some mysterious way, our bad habits lock themselves in, so efforts to defeat them only push us deeper into the mire. Willpower and mental effort usually make things worse in dealing with compulsions. Try as we will, we don't have what it takes to overcome these devilish problems.

Although the path of surrender seems hard and difficult, it is easier in the long run than the methods we have been using with such disastrous results. It is painful to admit one is an addict who needs help—but it is more painful to continue out of control behaviors. It may appear humiliating to become affiliated with a recovery group where people share their thoughts and feelings so openly. It is more humiliating to continue in the failure and degradation that can come with an active addiction. It also requires self-discipline and a firm resolve to attend meetings and to pay attention to the things necessary for growth in recovery. But this self-discipline is nothing compared with the vicious bondage we live under as slaves to addictions and other compulsions. We find true freedom, in fact, only when we surrender.

We surrender to win. The prizes are mental and physical health, true freedom, self-respect, serenity, confidence, health, and growth in happiness. With so much to win, the only mystery is why it took some of us so long to give up!

HUMILITY

HUMILITY IS A FREQUENT TOPIC AT MEETINGS OF recovering people, and is often difficult to talk about. This pamphlet will discuss some ideas about humility that may help us understand its role in recovery, and make it easier to talk about. Through understanding humility, we will learn to live and cope with abstinence and recovery.

Low Self-Worth/Big Ego

Let's take a look at the relationship between humility and low self-worth and what is commonly known as "big ego." Harry Tiebout, a close friend of Bill Wilson's and an early supporter of Alcoholics Anonymous, characterized the alcoholic as "king baby." By this, he meant that practicing addicts demand what they want when they want it and believe the universe revolves around them and their needs. Therefore, he concluded that continuing recovery depends upon maintaining awareness of our powerlessness over an addictive substance or behavior and the unmanageable quality of our lives.

The king baby quality of addicts is readily apparent in grandiose behavior. Addicts or codependents who spend money they don't have on people they hardly know or on things they don't need manifest grandiosity. Fantasizing future greatness or giving a gift instead of love are characteristics of grandiosity.

What may not be so apparent is that extreme low self-esteem is also a manifestation of the king baby quality. In a grandiose phase, a person considers him- or herself to be above others. However, extreme low self-esteem places one below others. In both instances, the person's attitude is "but I am different." Low self-esteem can also be a means of justifying self-centeredness, manipulating others through one's self-hatred, and constantly putting down oneself. There is the attitude of "I can do everything," and at the same time, "I can't do anything." Humility cuts through these two extremes with the recognition that "I can do something" with the help of a greater Power.

A Willingness to Learn

The ego state manifested in big ego or in low self-worth is in some ways a refusal on our part to admit we need help or that we can learn from others. No matter how long we have been in the program, we can continue to learn more about ourselves, others, and our Higher Power.

Believing a Power greater than ourselves can restore us to sanity is an acknowledgment that we are not experts on how to stay abstinent or how to live with an addict. In short, we need help in order to live and grow. We needed others to help us begin recovery. And as we continue to grow, even after years in the program, we still need others to help us maintain recovery.

In recovery, willingness to learn can expand beyond learning how to stay abstinent or how to live with an addict. Willingness to learn can become an ongoing acceptance of our limitations. If we let go of our prejudices, we can discover that learning how to live is not limited to experts or to people of our own race, sex, or socioeconomic class. Our ability to learn in life and to grow in recovery may be facilitated by anyone we meet in the program or outside of it.

Willingness to go to meetings, read literature about recovery, and spend time with a sponsor in honest sharing are helping us stay humble and abstinent. But we must also acknowledge and be willing to learn from our mistakes. The sadness that results from making mistakes is that often we fail to learn from them. As we grow in recovery, we learn more and more to accept responsibility for the consequences of our actions. Willingness to learn from mistakes can turn catastrophes into opportunities.

Humility and Humor

Humility and a sense of humor are closely related, but not in the sense that one can laugh at a cartoon or a funny story. It is an ability to laugh at oneself, and not take oneself too seriously. Before recovery began, many of us had suffered humiliations and saw nothing funny about them. But in the process of recovery, we began to laugh with others at some of our weaknesses and foibles. It is always easy to take ourselves too seriously, no matter how long we have been in the program. Twelve Step friends who continue to puncture our balloons of grandiosity or lift us out of the depths of self-pity with their humor are an important part of humility.

A person caught up in grandiose behavior may cause others to laugh. But you can be sure that person will be taking his or her actions very seriously. Likewise, someone who is in the throes of self-condemnation, self-hatred, and guilt will find little or nothing funny about his or her situation. In the process of recovery, as humility becomes one of the foundations of our lives, we begin to laugh at our past and even our present. This does not mean we are being irresponsible. It simply means we are seeing ourselves in perspective, and our actions, thoughts, and feelings may not be the center of the universe.

A Characteristic of the Program

Humility is a characteristic of the Twelve Step program and touches on each of the Steps. However, if we look at the Twelve Steps as a whole, we begin to see that working the program leads to a new way of perceiving ourselves in the world. We are no longer focused on our addiction or codependency. The escape from this was not a decision made on our own. I know of no one who woke up one morning and said, "It is a beautiful day. I have lots of money in the bank. My spouse and children love and respect me, and we have a fine relationship. I have good friends and meaningful work. I think I will stop this insanity and start going to meetings.''

For most of us the program becomes an escape from a life characterized by pain, fear, frustration, anger, and an attempt to have things our way. The Twelve Steps are a process of de-centering and re-centering our lives. As we know, self-centeredness in its various forms is at the root of our problem. The Steps give us a way of getting off dead center where our own desires, feelings, and demands are the focal point of our lives.

In living the program with the help of others, we continually make the discovery that the less self-centered we become, the more full our lives are and the more rewarding recovery is. The process of re-centering our lives on what we can give to others and how we can share what we have received is indeed a quality of life that can be called humble. It does not mean we are unconcerned about ourselves. However, the remarkable thing is that the more we re-center on other people and their needs, the more we receive.

It seems to be true, however, that this re-centering process means we also need to re-center our lives in relationship to our Higher Power. As we do this, we are more able to let go of others and serve them without trying to control and meet our own demands under the guise of helping. The re-centering of our lives in relationship to our Higher Power gives us a new freedom regarding others. Humility in this regard helps us maintain the perspective that reminds us we are not God, but are free to become fully human beings. In this sense, the program of the Twelve Steps leads indirectly to humility. Humility cannot be bought. Nor can it be directly decided upon. Humility is acquired indirectly through working the Steps, and leads to a healthy acceptance of self.

This may be a phenomenon of the Twelve Step program. It does not belong to a school of spirituality that says, "Are your spiritual muscles flabby? If so, take our special ten-day course and develop those muscles so that you are a spiritual or emotional giant or a very together person, and then you can take credit for it." The paradox of growth in working the Steps is that we cannot do it alone, yet no one can do it for us. Working the Twelve Steps not only leads to and requires humility, it also leads to a deeper and more secure sense of self-esteem. It is then that the joy in living we had originally sought becomes a reality.

Patience and Self-Acceptance

Humility looks different on different people, and often we have a false picture of what it is. We think of people walking with downcast eyes, never having anything good to say about themselves, and never acknowledging they are capable of anything. This is an erroneous picture of humility, although it is one that we frequently find ourselves believing. Instead, humility will differ for each of us, and we will become more humble as we become more who we really are.

Becoming who we truly are is not the same thing as asking ourselves the question, who am I? Frequently we think "identity crisis" means a close examination of our past in a very analytical way. The tendency to search for our uniqueness (as though it were some sort of reality we could find through continued self-searching) is the result of a mistaken idea of what our identity and humility really are.

Humility helps us recognize that we are both unique and ordinary, sharing all things that are important with the rest of humanity. The search for identity does not go back into the past as much as it goes forward into the future. This search asks who we want to become and how we can get there. Likewise, humility is not a continual dredging up of our past behavior, but rather a simple acceptance of our past, and a realization that we do not have to behave as we did before.

Perhaps some examples will help. Consider the accomplished musician who has worked very hard learning to play an instrument and then denies that he or she is good; or the man who has worked at his golf game and then continues to put himself down; or the person who gives a very good speech but continues to deny that he or she has a gift for speaking. Such a denial of gifts makes others as uncomfortable as being with someone who exaggerates his or her talents. Denial of our gifts and the inflation of the importance of our gifts are not characteristic of humility.

Humility looks different on different people because we have different gifts. To be humble is not to deny that one is gifted, but to acknowledge that our gifts make us a part of humanity rather than setting us up as superior to others. Nor do our limitations set us apart, they join us together, and we experience them as a source of unity rather than barriers of separation.

Steps Six and Seven

One of the most important insights of the Twelve Steps is that an addict or a codependent is a good person. Step Six acknowledges very realistically that we have defects of character. This is quite different from feeling we are defective characters. Even in moments of grandiosity, many of us have had the feeling there is something deeply wrong with us, that we are fatally flawed human beings, created somehow different and slightly out of place. This idea of being defective at the very core of our being is contrary to the Twelve Steps. However, we may have many defects of character that have been a source of disharmony and pain in our lives. If we look closely, we may discover our defects of character hurt ourselves more than anyone else.

We sometimes hear it said when we are making a list of people we have harmed by our addictive or compulsive behavior, that we should put ourselves at the top. This may be true, but the best way we can make amends to ourselves is by allowing the defects of character to be removed. Envy, greed, anger, jealousy, gluttony, pride, and lust may have blocked us from a more effective life. They have denied us a harmony with others, our Higher Power, and ourselves. As the defects of character are removed, we become more who we really are.

In Steps Six and Seven we first become ready to have these defects removed, and that means we have acknowledged they exist. What is meant by *entirely ready* is not necessarily to be interpreted as *wildly enthusiastic*. Rather, it means we are willing to undertake the difficult but rewarding path of spiritual growth, and to do this we need help from God as we understand Him.

Entirely ready means we will "never say never" about any defect.

Perhaps the main point Steps Six and Seven make regarding humility is that we need to continue to ask for help in the process of recovery. They also remind us that, although a defect of character may be removed, the capacity for it is not removed. If we are viewing defects of character as patterns of behavior which are a source of pain in our lives, then we must remember that even though the behavior may change, we retain a capacity for that kind of behavior.

For example, developing a way of life that demands rigorous honesty is a difficult and lifetime process. No matter how long we have been in the program or how honest we have become, this defect of dishonesty may continue to hinder our growth. At times we may have used honesty as a means of being brutal with other people, or we may find that we are being dishonest in our words, actions, gestures, or in the way we look at someone.

Around this defect of dishonesty, we see that we tend to use the same rationalizations as we always have. If we do not continue to take personal inventory and ask to have these defects removed, they can block our growth in recovery. We retain the capacity for our defects just as we retain the capacity to go back to old negative behaviors again, even though the desire to do this may have been lifted. We should not be surprised when even after years of recovery, defects of character continue to be a part of our lives. Remember Steps Six and Seven remain available to us as a way of continuing to make amends.

Achieving Humility

The Twelfth Tradition of a Twelve Step program also provides an important insight into another aspect of humility. It says anonymity is the spiritual foundation of our traditions, reminding us to place principles above personalities. The tradition of anonymity protects the group, as well as the individual. If we begin to apply the Twelfth Tradition to ourselves, we may see values in terms of personal growth.

A kind act done for someone which nobody finds out about, not even the person for whom it was done, can be a good way of checking where we are in terms of humility. If we find ourselves resisting doing those things for which there is little or no credit or expression of gratitude, we can begin to work on doing them and help our recovery process.

Developing gratitude as a way of life helps us grow in humility because we see life from a different perspective. We begin to notice in our lives all of the things we have to be grateful for on any given day. Also, by learning to be continually grateful and seeing not only recovery but other things in life as gifts, we recognize more fully what has been given rather than what has been achieved.

Another avenue to humility is the development of a sense of awe. This is closely related to gratitude but not quite the same. Some of us may live in places that are awe-inspiring, and yet we have taken them for granted. The sunset, a night sky in the winter, really looking at our children or lover, perhaps simply taking time to allow ourselves to appreciate the face of a friend, can help us develop a sense of awe. Awe takes us out of ourselves in a healthy way. Also, going to meetings, becoming involved in the service work, making coffee, being a greeter, going on Twelfth Step calls, listening to and sharing with others are all ways in which we can develop a sense of service to others and grow in humility and recovery.

These simple practices of gratitude, awe, real participation in meetings, listening and sharing, all help us toward a healthy and happy recovery. Along the way they give us a better perspective on who we are and who we can become. They also help us cut through the grandiosity and low self-worth of an ego-centered life and lead us toward growth in humility.

WHEN
DOORS
CLOSE

THERE'S A SAYING THAT WHEN ONE DOOR CLOSES ANother always opens. This adage recognizes there are times when life seems to put obstacles in our paths, when all avenues appear blocked, and we're stuck. It also recognizes that such times can lead to new success and happiness, if we're only willing to look around and see what other doors are open to us. There is always at least one other door—often many. Feeling stuck is simply our perception of what's happening in our lives. When we change our perceptions, we discover we're not stuck at all.

Addiction and recovery are fine examples of closed and open doors. For years we used and abused drugs, overate, gambled, or tried to control people because that made us feel better about ourselves and our world. Then our addictions and compulsions turned on us. We could no longer find the pleasure or relief we used to find from them. For most of us, the doors seemed to close with a bang when we hit bottom.

When we hit bottom we didn't know what to do. We were stuck on the merry-go-round of use, denial, addiction, or compulsion. Our lives seemed permanently ruined; we were hopeless and helpless. We thought we had nowhere to turn. But we know now, looking back, that this perception was wrong.

Our despair somehow led us to the process of recovery. We may have sought help on our own, or our employer, the courts, or a loved one may have insisted we enter a treatment program. We may not even be sure how it happened, but it did. No matter how it happened, a door we hadn't even known was there suddenly opened, and we stepped through to a new, productive, and satisfying way of life.

When we first begin recovery, we get a new lease on life; it's as if we've been reborn. As our minds clear, we awaken to the opportunities around us that we're now ready to act on. We have the ability to pursue dreams we once only thought about.

We often expect only good things will happen to us now that we're abstinent, although the program certainly doesn't promise this. In fact, many people experience a "honeymoon" when they begin recovering. Many of our problems begin to clear up; we may reunite with our families; the employer who threatened to fire us may welcome us back to work. Our financial problems may clear up. We may find a new group of friends, and more importantly, have a new way of life that will bring the peace of mind we always wanted.

Eventually the honeymoon ends, however. As we go about our daily affairs and begin to live fuller lives, we find it doesn't all go smoothly. Open doors suddenly close in our faces.

For instance, we may feel ready to make a lucrative career change, but we discover the job isn't available or someone else was hired. Our heart may be set on moving to a new apartment or location, but we are unable to do so. Vacation or travel plans may be interrupted. We may think we've found our lifelong partner, only to have the romance end suddenly and unpleasantly. We often go through periods when all doors seem closed. Our best plans go awry, no matter how hard we work. Such times are incredibly frustrating.

The solution is to find the open door. Our own stories of addiction and recovery contain the keys to finding and opening new doors, and the Twelve Steps provide the method.

When a door closes, we can take constructive action rather than spending our emotions destructively. We can turn closed doors into powerful learning experiences. We can move ahead and stop spinning our wheels by drawing on the Twelve Steps. When we understand the circumstances around us, we can build a foundation that allows us to decide what to do next.

First Things First

Just as it was necessary to accept our disease before recovery could really begin, we must accept closed doors and recognize our powerlessness. Step One isn't limited to our addiction or compulsion; we can use it in any situation. The more we apply Step One, the less often we'll feel stuck.

If, for instance, we don't get a job we wanted, we can accept our powerlessness over the situation. The job isn't ours, no matter how much we wished for it, and there's nothing we can do about it. The job rejection can be used as an opportunity to increase our faith that our Higher Power has something better in store for us— a chance to practice Step Three.

This acceptance and surrender is necessary in any

situation: a move that didn't work out, a broken romance, or spoiled vacation plans. When we truly believe and turn our will and lives over to our Higher Power, we can be certain our lives will work.

When a door shuts in our faces, we're likely to feel depressed about it. Even if we have accepted the fact, we're apt to feel resentful. It's easy to think our efforts are pointless because nothing seems to work. The solution to this depression is action. Such action can be as simple as getting up and fixing breakfast or as complicated as going back to school. Attending more meetings and reaching out to help others are also cures for depression.

We can use Step Ten to inventory the situation. When doors shut in our faces we are upset because we are disappointed. It can help to understand what our expectations were. Taking a close look at our feelings and expectations—preferably in writing—is constructive action that clears up depression and points us toward the open door.

In the case of a job rejection, we might want to ask ourselves such questions as: Why did I expect to get that job? Did I misunderstand something the interviewer said? Did I assume I was qualified when perhaps I wasn't? Am I willing to admit the person who got the job was more qualified? Was I reaching too high, based on my qualifications and experience? Was I dealing in wishful thinking?

Questions like these put the failure in perspective, if we answer them honestly. The same kinds of questions work well in other circumstances.

Pride May Be a Problem

We shouldn't overlook pride in our inventories. When a door is shut, our egos are likely to be wounded. We're apt to feel we deserved better treatment. Maybe we've bragged to our friends about anticipated changes, and now we feel foolish having to admit we didn't get what we wanted. When we see pride getting in our way, we can use Step Seven and ask God to remove it.

We can also ask ourselves, is that job, apartment, or relationship what I truly needed? Or were these goals merely what I wished I had or thought I should have?

In the early stages of recovery, we often fall into the trap of doing what we think we should, rather than what we truly want to do. We may fool ourselves about the kind of work we want because it has prestige or offers a high salary. We may think moving to a particular area will enhance our image, even though we prefer a simpler life-style.

It rarely works to pursue goals only because we think we should, rather than because we truly want them. When things go wrong, we have an opportunity to look within ourselves and find our true objectives.

An inventory should include some positive things too. We may discover we want a particular job or place to live. An inventory can help us take a closer look at what we have to offer. Then we can turn apparent failure into success by deciding what needs to be done. For example, we may need more training or we may need to take a job that will allow us to work up the ladder. We may have to reassess how we're using our income, so our spending matches our priorities.

If we discover our objectives conflict with what we truly want, we can use this information to discover what our goals should be. Often we find clues to what we really want by looking at what we already do well. Once we know what we want, we can take the appropriate action to accomplish it.

In either case, we've taken the opportunity to find out more about ourselves, which is always an advantage.

Being Put on Hold

Other examples of doors closing are those periods when we feel as if we've been put on hold. We feel there's no movement in our lives. In the job world, it often means we wait for someone else to make a decision, so we know what to do next. Or, we apply for credit, and the bank takes longer than we think necessary to make a decision. Our love life seems stagnant—either we don't have a relationship or our current relationship is going through the doldrums. Even our program and spiritual growth seem to have hit a plateau.

It's tempting, but unwise, to force a resolution during these periods. If we try to kick a particular door open, we're likely to discover we've created more problems than we had in the first place. It's also tempting to give up and feel nothing is worth pursuing. This is also a dead-end street. We may give up just before achieving success.

The key to tolerating these periods is patience—sometimes lots of it. After we've done everything reasonable, we can only wait hopefully, gracefully, until the situation resolves itself.

A quick way to increase our patience is through practicing Step Eleven. Improving our conscious contact with our Higher Power will result in clarity and peace of mind. Prayer and meditation can take many forms. It doesn't always have to be a formal process. Walking in the woods, listening to calming music, or taking a long, relaxing shower will often still our minds and renew our sense of connection to our Higher Power.

We can also use Step Twelve to help us feel unstuck. Reaching out to others is a sure way to take our minds off ourselves. Working with others puts our own lives in perspective. Sharing our experience, strength, and hope helps us realize how far we've come in our recovery. These things get us out of ourselves and tend to stop the circular thinking that makes us so miserable. Even taking a job for our group such as being secretary or treasurer puts us back in the position of giving rather than receiving.

It's also helpful to talk about our frustrations at meetings and with our sponsors. When we share experiences, we'll find we're not alone; people who have gone through similar situations will be happy to share their experiences with us.

Doors We Close

Don't overlook the doors we close ourselves. It's easy to assume the door was closed by someone or something else. But often we close them without even realizing it. We may close a door by failing to follow up on an unexpected opportunity. Our recovery again provides a concrete example. Few of us, while acting compulsively, would have considered the threat of being fired or a conviction for drunk driving to be opportunities for recovery. But these negative situations can work out well. If we refuse chances, we might shut the door on a new and satisfying way of life.

The same is true of other situations in our lives. We may meet someone who says he or she has a job for us.

If we don't follow through, we'll never know what kind of opportunity we missed. Someone may suggest we would enjoy living in a neighborhood we never considered before. If we don't at least take a look, we may pass up the perfect location. We may get stuck in a rut of only going to certain weekly meetings. Trying a new meeting may open up a whole new view of our program. We'll never know until we try.

Each day is like a new door opening. We can either say yes and walk through, or refuse and shut the door. If we're alert, open-minded, and willing, we'll be able to see the doorways open to us. We need to be flexible and resourceful, rather than stuck in our preconceived notions of how life should be.

Summing Up

There are times when doors close—it's a fact of life. We don't need to expect them to close, but we shouldn't be surprised when it happens.

And it's true that when one door closes, another always opens. We simply have to be willing to look, often in new directions, to find the open door.

Our recovery makes it possible for us to look for the newly opened door, to take advantage of it, and to walk through it in confidence. Just as we found the courage to walk through the open door of recovery, we can find the courage to turn our backs on closed doors and move on.

Staying alert and working Steps Ten, Eleven, and Twelve will assure our continued growth in the program and in our lives.

UNDERSTANDING
REJECTION

THE PAIN OF REJECTION CAN BE UNBEARABLE. I'LL never forget the woman who called me one midnight on the hotline. She was high and asked me my name. I told her, but when I asked her name, she replied, "Zero."

"No, no," I said, "your name is not Zero. You don't have to tell me what it is, but I have to tell you it's not Zero because you are a person, a valuable human being. You have a real name. God loves you."

She was silent.

"Listen, I know how you feel," I went on, "I've been there. But that was eighteen months ago and I'm okay now; I'm in recovery. I'm in a Twelve Step program. I'm glad you called because I can tell you I know there's hope for you. God has hope for you. Talk to me."

She began her story. It was the familiar story of despair. She had no friends, no family, no job, no money. She had suffered a total loss of self-esteem. She had lost all hope. She wanted to die.

The pain of all that rejection was in her voice, a voice filled with grief and tears and mourning for herself.

A Tangle of Emotions

Rejection isn't easy under any circumstances. For the addict who may be either feeling rejected or dishing rejection out, rejection is a difficult emotion because it is so entangled with other tough emotions.

When we feel rejected, we also feel certain fears and begin discounting ourselves. In self-defense, the beginning of resentment arises.

But, when we reject others it becomes another story; it becomes anger. According to a psychiatrist I once saw, anger is supposed to be okay when it is righteous. "Righteous anger is okay," she said.

I wasn't in the program then. I had not yet tried to perform the ultimate rejection upon myself that finally led me to the program and recovery. I was still in heavy denial which was rejection of myself, my addiction, my God, and any hope for help. Talk about righteous anger.

In our recovery, we want to be perfect. But, we learn we are not perfect and never will be perfect. With this in mind, we can sort through our anger and ask ourselves when anger is okay. When can we be angry about feeling rejected? When can anger be the instrument by which we can legitimately reject others?

We don't know much about the woman who called herself Zero, yet we can identify with her if we have ever been where she was the night she called the hotline and said she was going to have to kill herself.

She was communicating ultimate rejection. It is the place some of us, in our insanity, arrive at after all the other rejections we have received and given in our lives. We may have thought we should just get on with it and get it over with. But in recovery, we have to know and firmly believe this ultimate kind of rejection is no longer an option and never was.

Sometimes we need to remind ourselves that suicide is no option, no matter how painful the reminder. When we pause and give some thought to this, we are then able to help others. And helping others is a vital part of our recovery.

The Ultimate Dialogue

When the woman called the hotline that night, it presented the opportunity for the ultimate dialogue—a response to her rejection of herself and her rotten world. That call gave me an opportunity to work with God and let God direct the conversation in trying to save a life. I was given the opportunity to tell her why staying alive is the only way to fight rejection. And I told her how we can find hope by going to meetings and being with others who are in the same boat we are.

At first she wasn't buying my words. But she called back several times throughout the night until she finally said, ''I give up,'' and hung up the phone. It was two-way rejection: First, she rejected my words; then, she rejected herself.

However, she called again. She'd had a nap. By the sound of her voice, she was higher than before. The dialogue went on until it was agreed I would call her in the morning. In the morning, my calls were unanswered. The lifeline seemed to be closed forever, and I felt rejected.

This, however, isn't the end of the story. Even though we'll never really know about the person who called herself Zero, we can't give up hope. Maybe she went to a meeting that morning. Maybe she heard the message and decided to try living one more time. Maybe she's still alive.

We can't give up on ourselves or on those who are still addicted. We're all in the same boat. We can't stop fighting rejection for a moment—whether it's ours or someone else's—because it is a mistake we can't afford.

As practicing addicts we used to feel rejected in an amazingly routine way. We felt angrily rejected when the paperboy didn't deliver the paper on time. *So we got drunk.* We felt rejected when our two-year-old son didn't want a kiss. *So we gorged on food.*

We felt rejected when our mother didn't call to see how we were, or when a good friend failed to invite us to a party. We felt rejected when someone at the party frowned when he saw us pour yet another hefty drink or bet money on a football game. We felt rejected again and again, so *we went back to our addictions.*

Rejection also works in the reverse direction. We proclaim, "To hell with the newspaper. I'll cancel it and get a different paper." "To hell with my child; someone else will kiss me." "As for you, dear mother, you seem to forget I called you when you needed me. But I won't do that again, because you don't care about me."

These were the reasons we gave for acting out of control. It's hard to believe these types of reasons now, isn't it? It's hard to believe we used to be that way, offering an open invitation to rejection in endless situations. But, in some ways we're still there. *We're not perfect.* We can remember that rejection can sometimes be a valid emotion with us, if we examine it and make it a positive outcome rather than a negative outlook.

Positive Responses to Rejection

We need to hear the music of a Twelve Step program because it is a symphony for us. It is life itself. It is a twelve-note chord, a musical score. When it is translated into a program for life, it is a blueprint for recovery. We need to turn rejection around in our thoughts and use it positively.

If we wonder if this is possible, we can look at our lives and realize we *have* done this. In recovery we have rejected the option of ever going back to our old way of life again. We have rejected suicide. We have rejected dishonesty, disrespect, fear, grandiosity, unrealistic expectations, loneliness, impatience, and paranoia. We have done this *one day at a time*.

And by doing this, by rejecting the negatives in our lives, we have learned to accept the positive aspects of ourselves and others. Thus, some forms of rejection aren't so bad after all. Some righteous anger or rejection is okay. It goes back to the matter of sorting things out.

Some of us may be feeling rejected right now. Maybe we're having a problem sorting out feelings about ourselves or someone else who is important in our lives. We may feel inadequate or lonely. We may feel impatient, even angry with ourselves. We may feel lost and confused.

These feelings are okay. We're human. We can relax, quiet ourselves, and say the Serenity Prayer.

We can take a few minutes right now, wherever we are, and review the program and its miraculous Twelve Steps. We can remember how they helped us begin our recovery and stay with it, one step at a time, one day at a time.

We can remember the First Step, our heavy denial, and how we finally rejected that denial and began to admit our powerlessness. We can remember the Second and Third Steps where we began to accept ourselves and our defects; we let our Higher Power into our lives to help us learn to deal with those defects and our new lives.

When we're still, we can listen to the music of the program, and we know we're not alone. Again and again, the reprise tells us we are one among many who have, at one time or another, experienced something close to ultimate rejection.

We can no longer reject ourselves with the kind of misplaced sensitivity and loneliness that drinking brought us. God is with us.

The Larceny of Rejection

Maybe there is something to that old saying about everyone having a little larceny in their souls. Larceny is cribbing, cheating, and deceiving for self-gain. When we felt rejected, we drank or binged and this became the theft of our personal goals, happiness, and self-respect. This was larcenous behavior, and we robbed ourselves.

In recovery, we have stopped robbing ourselves and started to look at feelings behind that rejection. Perhaps we feel *discounted*. That's a valid word and feeling, and we may feel discounted for a legitimate reason.

We need to remember that ''stinkin' thinkin' '' is larcenous behavior. It can sneak up on us and quickly undermine our recovery. A negative outlook can cause us to substitute one bad habit for another, denying the problem. We may have said to ourselves or to our friends, ''No more whiskey for me. I'll drink wine or beer. Then I'll be okay.''

These ways of substitution only make our negative feelings escalate. For example, consider Bob, who telephoned an insurance company to take care of some important business for him. The person Bob needed to talk with wasn't there. He left a message asking that person to return his call as soon as possible. After a few days passed with no answer, he asked himself if he felt rejected, but he told himself this emotion was not *allowed*. But he did feel discounted. He felt the person he called wasn't giving him the respect he deserved. He even jumped to conclusions, thinking people who deserved less attention than he were getting better service.

We get so entangled in our feelings sometimes that the end result is a feeling of rejection. We can call it hurt, neglect, ignorance, indifference, hatred, or even being discounted wholesale. In the end, it is rejection. That's the feeling, and we need to sort it out while it's happening to us. We need to think very carefully and thoughtfully about all the reasons we used in concluding we'd been rejected. We need to go beyond these feelings to all the perfectly good reasons why that person didn't call us back.

We can also experience Bob's reaction in our personal relationships. If friends are slow in returning calls, they may have forgotten. Rather than feeling rejected, we can remember our friends may have legitimate reasons for not calling us back.

We need to be as understanding of others as we want them to be of us. But, if we could always do that we might not have to take the time to read this pamphlet. We're not perfect; we're human. The only *perfect being* is our Higher Power who is very much with us right now.

Gratitude

We may never know what happened to the woman who called herself Zero. She may have performed the ultimate rejection on herself, or she may have found a Twelve Step program. The most important thing for us to know is that we're alive. We will not ever reject ourselves again because of our addiction or compulsion. God is with us. Thank God we're with Him.

We thank God every morning, every night, sometimes every hour of the day, for our recovery. We thank our Higher Power for being with us at all times as we continue to maintain, or struggle to maintain, our recovery. We thank our Higher Power for helping us work through the many emotions that sometimes get in our way, knowing that He will help us see those same emotions from a different point of view—a vantage point—that is entirely positive.

We live in a difficult world, a world of conflicts. Yet, we do not have to think entirely in terms of opposing forces. We don't have to substitute love for hate, love for jealousy, or love for anger. This approach doesn't necessarily work. There are no absolutes in the world of emotions.

Rejection can be difficult to deal with whether it is real or imagined. The important thing right now is to care about ourselves as rational human beings by thinking carefully about whether or not we have really been rejected. If we decide we have, we can do something positive about it. We can accept the rejection, sort through it, and turn it over to God.

How we handle rejection is extremely important. As recovering people, we turn to the Twelve Step program and the support system of our recovery, and we work things out with the help of others who understand us. One of those who understands us is our Higher Power. He knows and understands us best. May we find Him now.

FREEDOM
FROM
FEAR

It MAY HAVE BEEN YEARS SINCE WE'VE FELT THE FEAR that permeated our days as practicing addicts. We may have experienced something of the new freedom and happiness promised by the program of the Twelve Steps. Yet fear may remain a problem for us. At times fear may try to dominate us again and we may react in the same old ways and wonder if we have made any progress at all. Responding to fear in constructive ways is an important dimension of ongoing recovery.

Fear and Denial

When we find ourselves burdened by resentments, if we look behind them we may discover fear in various forms. It may be the fear of not getting what we feel we want or need. It may be the fear of losing something or someone. Fear of loss of prestige or loss of self-image may result in deep anger at anything that seems to attack us. What we often call our perfectionism is sometimes nothing more than a desire to be beyond criticism. The desire to control the lives of those around us may really be a fear of acknowledging our powerlessness. As we attempt to develop a way of living which demands rigorous honesty, we may be forced again and again to acknowledge the reality of fear in our lives.

Fear causes the most trouble for us when we pretend we have none or when we think our lives can be totally free from fear. Fear is not a defect of character. If we were deprived of our capacity for fear we would be robots, not heroes. The goal of the Twelve Steps is not to destroy our human capacity for fear, but rather to transform our responses to fear and eventually change the nature of them.

An example might help clarify the importance of fear. There are some people who are born without the ability to feel physical pain. At first, this might seem like a blessing. But as these people have been studied, or as anyone who lives with them can report, the lack of capacity for pain is a curse. As children, they need to be watched more carefully than children who feel pain. A child who feels pain will withdraw a hand from a burning oven. But a child incapable of feeling pain does not have that immediate instinct of withdrawal and can be seriously burned.

Growing into adulthood, people unable to feel pain have no way of knowing whether they are hurt or suffering from some illness. Pain, which is a symptom of illness, doesn't register for them. They can become seriously ill, not know it, and not seek adequate help. A person incapable of feeling pain may be as seriously hindered from living a full human life as the person who suffers from chronic pain. Likewise, a person with no fear in any situation might have as much difficulty living as one whose life is dominated by fear.

We have all heard the phrase "I'm feeling no pain."

That was often what we were seeking as a permanent condition through our addictive behavior. We may at times have sought a way of escaping or confronting our fears by acting out our addictive behavior. In ongoing recovery we are learning to accept the roles of pain and fear in our lives. The capacity and the experience of fear on occasion are important factors in helping us develop as recovering human beings.

Fight, Flight, or Freeze

In the early 1900s Dr. William Cannon did some research on what has been called the "fight or flight" mechanism. He discovered that most animals, when confronted with a dangerous situation, have an almost immediate reaction of either fighting back or fleeing from the danger. This fight or flight mechanism also seems to be part of our human reaction to things, people, and situations we fear.

Dr. Cannon also noted that almost all animals, when faced with a dangerous situation they cannot interpret, simply freeze and don't move at all. We all have probably come across a squirrel or rabbit while walking and noticed that when it becomes aware of our presence it freezes for a moment. If we take a step toward it, the animal will dart off to the nearest tree or clump of bushes. It seems that in our own case as recovering people, fear can cause us to fight, flee, or even become paralyzed.

The fight, flight, or freeze mechanism is intended as a short term response to a particular dangerous situation. We can, however, respond in these ways over a long period of time and do tremendous damage to ourselves as well as those around us. For example, someone may consistently refuse promotions which are really wanted because of a fear of failure or fear of responsibility. Another person may remain paralyzed in a relationship that is destructive because of the fear of being on one's own. Another person may live a life characterized by arguments and disagreements that are out of proportion to the cause. Extended over a considerable time period, these reactions to fear not only cause considerable stress, but they deprive us of the fullness of recovery. Before recovery, our fear may have progressed to a point where we met every situation frightened of what could go wrong. In recovery we gradually learn to overcome our fear of people, or of doing things we had always wanted to do but didn't have the courage. Gradually we learn to meet a situation, not in terms of the fear of it, but in terms of its potential. Through the program, we can begin to discern clearly what our fears are and what our initial responses to them may be. We learn that by sharing our fears with others, no matter how petty or irrational those fears may seem, we can make decisions regarding our fear rather than simply reacting to it.

Again, let it be noted that some fears are very healthy. For example, the fear of relapsing is healthy because we know returning to our former ways would be self-destructive. In this case, fear may be a motivator in keeping us abstinent. Even in the healthiest people there remains a fear of relapsing. But over the long run, fear will not keep us abstinent.

Fear of Failure

Perhaps if we look back at some of our actions before recovery, we might discover we were not motivated by a desire for success, but rather by fear of failure. When fear of failure is coupled with expectations that are too high, it can cause us to refuse opportunities we may wish to take, paralyze us in the middle of a new venture, or lead us to pour our energies into avoiding failure rather than succeeding. All these fears rob us of the joy of achievement. Fear of failure, or of appearing to be a failure, can haunt us well into recovery. It may even block us in our program, for example, by a fear of giving a talk when we are asked.

Fear of failure may be healthy when it keeps us from undertaking ventures we are not suited for, or when it tempers our grandiosity. Not wanting to see an undertaking fail is a normal and healthy reaction and may provide motivation for working harder. The question is, how do we know when our fear of failure is realistic and healthy and when it is unhealthy fear blocking our growth and dominating our lives? One way of deciding whether our fear is realistic or unhealthy is to discuss it honestly with somebody else. If we hear ourselves saying, "I don't want to talk about it," then it is likely our fear is an unhealthy one.

Willingness to discuss our fear honestly with another person in the program gives us good insight. Frequently we may find we are victims of false fears which will melt away in the face of our own honesty. We may discover our fears are normal and shared by other people, and need to be worked on.

It is important to remember that the final decision, whether to listen to a particular fear or not, is our own. A person trying to decide whether or not to return to school may discover a great deal of fear surrounding that decision. By sharing this fear the person may realize such fears are normal and shared by many other students. Sharing fear lessens its power over us and gives us the strength to proceed with a decision even though some of the fear may remain. Knowing we are not alone and that we are not the first person to be in a position to make such a decision can give us the strength we need.

Someone struggling with a decision whether or not to accept a new position might discover, through sharing fears of a job change with another person, that these fears are authentic and maybe there is good reason not to proceed with this particular change. The person may discover that he or she is considering making a change not because it is wanted, but because of the fear of how it would look if it were refused. The person may have legitimate fears regarding what such a move would mean to self, family, and ongoing recovery. By sharing these fears with others it becomes possible to make better decisions. A person deciding whether or not to speak at a meeting may discover that the fear is indeed genuine and that he or she is not quite ready. By sharing fears, one may discover there are other things to do. For example, one could speak up more at discussion meetings, go out with the group after a meeting and do some talking, or perhaps even take a speaking class to lessen the fears and provide opportunity for growth.

The point to all of this is that as we share fear of failure with other people, a number of good things can happen. We have a firmer foundation for making good decisions. We become able to listen to our fears and respond to them rather than simply react, and we run less risk of being dominated by them.

Fear of Rejection

Another major source of fear for many people is the fear of rejection. This particular fear is normal, to be expected in the course of recovery, and may pop up when we are least prepared. It is one of the most difficult fears in life to deal with; however, it is not impossible. It is a familiar fear to most of us. At any time, it can loom up as one of the major roadblocks to the fullness of life.

In its extreme forms, fear of rejection may lead us to being overly aggressive in our relationships. As an extension of the fight syndrome, it may lead us to keep others away, by constantly battling with them and not giving them an opportunity to reject us. As an extension of the flight syndrome, we may avoid giving people an opportunity to really get to know us because we fear they won't like us if they know who we really are. The fear of rejection may lead us to extremes of "people pleasing." It may even cause us to do things we would rather not do.

There is no neat and simple way to deal with fear of rejection. The fact is, most of us learn to handle it the hard way by being rejected and discovering we can survive it. Perhaps the best way to work through fear of rejection is by becoming aware of the pain that fear itself causes, and to be aware that this fear is more painful than the actual rejection. If we allow ourselves to be dominated by the fear of rejection, we actually reject ourselves, and this is more painful than having someone else not accept us. Again, sharing our fear with others can lessen this fear and enable us to take a chance and grow in healthy ways.

How to Deal With Our Fears

Perhaps the best advice regarding fear comes directly from the Big Book of Alcoholics Anonymous. It says, "We reviewed our fears thoroughly. We put them on paper, even though we had no resentment in connection with them." Fear belongs in our inventory on a regular basis. The reason is that fears, even those which may be healthy, may be the source of self-pity, resentment, and dishonesty. The fear of not getting what we want, of losing something we have, or of not looking good are all normal fears and do not disappear simply because we no longer use. Indeed, they can be so subtle that they can enter our lives at any point. Willingness to share our fears is an effective and practical way of dealing with them. As we have noted, the very act of sharing a fear may cause it to melt away or give us new insight to deal with it. Fear, unattended and unshared, will grow and become more of a problem.

The regular practice of prayer and meditation is a way of becoming free from our fears. The Big Book recommends the practice of short prayers in times of stress which ask for guidance and indicate a willingness to let go. Many people find that saying the serenity prayer or just thinking about it can alleviate a momentary fear. For fears and anxieties that may be deeper, the regular practice of meditation for twenty minutes or more a day may have significant long-term effects. Returning to a passage from a favorite meditation book or the slow, quiet, and unharried repetition of a favorite phrase may help us not only improve our conscious contact with God as we understand Him, but also bring about a sense of serenity that alleviates our fears.

Responses to Fear

We are seeking in recovery not to be free from the capacity for fear, but rather to become free from fear which dominates our lives or interferes with the fullness of our growth and development. As we become aware of fear and face it, we have more freedom of choice in how we respond to it, but this requires courage. The word *courage* is derived from the Latin word *cor* which means "heart." Thus, to encourage someone is to "en-hearten"—to put heart into him or her. To discourage someone, then, means to take the heart out. Fear can discourage us. It can take the heart out of our lives and our recovery. So we need to discover and cultivate sources of encouragement. We may find this in the Twelve Steps and in people in recovery programs. We may discover sources of encouragement through new activities as well as through prayer and meditation. We may even discover courage within ourselves.

Courage may show itself by our willingness to take a small step in the face of fear rather than an overwhelmingly big step we cannot make. Our willingness to take a risk in the face of our fear is no small matter. Sharing that triumph can provide us with the foundation for further steps and also serve to encourage those around us. Acknowledging the progress we have made in becoming free from the fear that dominated our lives is a source not only of gratitude, but of courage and faith in meeting present fears.

As in recovery, there is a gift dimension to faith. Just as we grow and develop in recovery so, too, we may grow in faith. Faith is simply the open willingness to receive help. For some, growth in faith is slow and steady. For many of us, growth is occasioned by pain and feelings of fear or resentment. The faith and trust we thought had freed us from fear begins to seem fragile. But as one old timer in the program said, "God did not get us into recovery just to throw us back." We can have faith that our Higher Power will turn the crisis into opportunity.

"Freedom from fear" means being free from a life dominated by fear, rather than being free from the capacity for it. Fear can play a healthy role in the growth of our recovery. When fear leads us to a "fight, flight, or freeze" reaction it can be harmful, and this is most likely to happen through fear of failure or fear of rejection. A regular inventory of the role of fear in our lives keeps us from denying that fear exists. Sharing our fears with others can be the source of courage and faith we need to meet them. Prayer and meditation are ways of sharing our fears with our Higher Power and transforming them. The program of the Twelve Steps does indeed promise us new freedom and happiness and the freedom from fear for life.

LONELINESS

LONELINESS IS PART OF BEING HUMAN. NO ONE IS exempt. There are times when, no matter how strong our faith is, or how much spiritual or personal growth we've experienced, loneliness will flood our lives. The loss of a loved one, the critical illness of a child, making a tough decision, supporting an unpopular position, and sometimes just doing what we know to be right can isolate us from others in a painful and yet unavoidable way. Sometimes we can find no direct trigger for our feelings—we just feel disconnected from the flow of life around us.

We may be tempted to escape the discomfort by running to work, friends, or activities in the same way we used to run to chemicals, food, sex, or other compulsions. While this may provide some temporary relief, it usually increases our sense of isolation. As is true with any emotion, the attempt to deny or control the isolation will only give it more power. The willingness to experience what we are feeling often reduces the intensity of the feeling.

While few would consider loneliness enjoyable, it can

encourage us to reach out to others, and to seek a power beyond. Calling our sponsor or a friend, getting to a meeting, and sharing our pain can help us get out of ourselves in a healthy way. Reading recovery or inspirational literature may help us regain a sense of perspective. If we have suffered a major loss or are feeling grief, we may be able to find a support group which deals with that specific issue.

Many recovering people lead such busy and full lives that the feelings of loneliness may be coming from isolation from themselves. The solution might be to spend more time on ourselves. We may need to schedule daily time when we can center and work on our daily recovery program. We may be spending so much time and energy on work and service that we don't leave any quality time to spend with family and friends. We need to protect our mutually nurturing relationships by continuing to invest ourselves in them.

The paradoxical nature of loneliness is not new to recovering people. Before recovery, we believed we were unique and beyond the understanding of mere mortals. Yet, we could not honestly let others know who we were, for we did not know ourselves. We would swing from a grandiosity that told us we were better than others to a deep sense of shame which made us feel unworthy of any relationships. We drove people away, felt rejected by them, and then rejected ourselves. While believing our addiction or compulsion would solve all our problems, we defiantly denied the existence of any Power greater than ourselves.

Our journey away from loneliness is equally filled with paradox. We learn we are neither perfect saints nor perfect sinners. We are simply human. Although we are capable of great wrongs, there is also a basic goodness in each of us. As we begin to accept ourselves and others, we discover it frequently is by sharing our weaknesses and vulnerability that we gain mutual understanding and connectedness. By sharing our powerlessness and brokenness with others, we are confronted with the need of a Power for good, for unity, for healing—a Power greater than our mutual selves—to restore us to a sense of belonging.

The Twelve Steps and the fellowship of recovery groups bring us into a relationship of harmony and connectedness with ourselves, others, and God. These relationships lead us from aloneness to solitude and from isolation to community. As we look at some of the ways in which this restoration occurs, we must keep in mind that it is not an either/or proposition. We cannot be reconciled with ourselves unless we are also working toward healthy relationships with others.

Ourselves . . .

For those of us for whom a complicated lie was easier than a simple truth, who kept secrets not only from others but from ourselves as well, or who lied to God and knew it and lied about knowing it, getting honest is a formidable task. However, to reach a point where we are comfortable being alone, we must come to know ourselves. We must replace our old lies of who we are and are not with some new, hard-fought-for truths. It is through working the inventory Steps that we begin to know who we really are.

The First Step tells us we are powerless and unmanageable. The Fourth Step shows us our strengths and weaknesses, our motives, feelings, and values. Many find it helpful to repeat the Fourth Step inventory periodically as we grow in honesty and as our insights change our understanding of our past.

A friend who had done her first Fourth Step at the end of her second year of recovery had great difficulty finding her shortcomings as she sifted through an overwhelming amount of negative emotion from childhood: pain, loss, grief, and fear. In a later inventory, she was amazed to find a tremendous amount of love given and received in that same childhood. She realized much of the remembered loneliness was self-inflicted through her childish demands and self-centeredness. She had believed others existed solely to meet her needs. Her efforts were rewarded with a new sense of healing of old memories as well as new freedom in her relationships today.

It may be helpful for us to do a special Fourth Step when loneliness becomes a problem. Do we have grief issues that are blocking intimacy? Were there some things we were unable to tell in our Fifth Step that are still fueling our sense of shame? When has loneliness been a problem in our lives before? What was happening in terms of situations and feelings? Can we see patterns emerging? What was our part in it? How can we use our program to work through this situation in a healthy way? What can we learn from it?

Recovery is slow, but as it continues we can see progress. In addition to admitting when we are wrong as we work our Tenth Step, we also need to admit our progress, to gratefully incorporate positive growth into ourselves. Sharing our developing understanding with a sponsor is a good way to reinforce our insights as well as to keep honest. Using a sponsor increases our sense of being okay, while being a sponsor increases our sense of usefulness.

Others . . .

We discover in recovery that we are not the self-sufficient creatures we once thought. For most of us, relearning how to establish satisfying relationships with others began at meetings. Our addiction and willingness to recover led us to a fellowship of people who understood and accepted us without reservation.

A friend tells of arriving at a Twelve Step meeting one night and being overcome by feelings of isolation and loneliness as he stood by the door watching the other members laughing and talking together. It was then that he knew, for the first time in his life, that he really belonged. This group of people was truly his family. Even if they ran away, he could run with them. He was not alone.

It is said that hearts are opened from the inside. For many of us in whom the sense of shame was so great that we were incapable of either venturing out to others or of receiving the warmth that was so freely offered, our hearts opened very slowly. It was in the environment of deep commitment to mutual recovery that we began to trust.

We are responsible for the hand of our recovery group to always be there, and that is a two-way responsibility for each of us. We must be willing to extend our hand to the newcomer, to share our experience, strength, and hope.

We must remember that we, too, are always "newcomers" in that we have only a daily reprieve from our illness—whether it be chemical dependency, overeating, sex addiction, or codependency. Where is our trust level today? Are we going to enough meetings? Are we bringing up our concerns when we get there? Are we still using our sponsor? Are we sharing our feelings of loneliness with others or is false pride keeping us in the role of "old-timer"? Unless we keep our group experience alive through active participation, it will become a memory which lacks the power to strengthen our lives today.

In order to extend to other relationships the feelings of comfort and connectedness we experience in the Fellowship, we must "practice these principles in all our affairs." We must bring that same openness and honesty, acceptance and trust, to our families and friends and into the workplace. What we learn about the human experience in recovery must become the basis of all our relationships. If we wish to feel connected to others, we must be willing to become vulnerable. We begin by making amends.

We may discover some real harm we have done in an active, concrete way or we may discover the harm came as a result of our unreasonable expectations or demands. We may have wanted others to have more power than humans are capable of and solve our problems. We may have wanted them to let us act as the "fixers" and controllers of their lives. When things didn't turn out the way we planned, we perhaps hurt both them and ourselves in our disappointment.

In making amends to others, we sometimes need to do a specific restitution, or give a verbal admission of wrong and an apology. Often, however, our amends must include a conscious amending of our view of the others. We come to a deep sense of relatedness when we can extend to all of the people in our lives the same right to be human, the same right to be wrong, that we extend to ourselves and to our recovering friends. The ability to acknowledge our common humanity, the ability to share our loneliness openly and honestly with another as a part of that common humanity, enables us to form true community.

God . . .

Few of us were on speaking terms with God when
we first came into the Program. We might not have
doubted that He could restore us to sanity, but feared
He wouldn't. Old understandings ranged from the
"white-robed, candy store man in the sky," somewhat passive and indulgent, to the "angry, punitive,
arbitrary judge" who accepts no excuses for not following the law to the letter. With few exceptions,
"God as we understood Him" was not someone to
whom we would want to turn over the care of our life
and our will.

Most of us reached a point in recovery when we could
no longer remain "unconscious" in our contact with
God. We had to bring the same rigorous honesty we
found so vital with self and others into our relationship
with our Higher Power. We came to believe that our
unwillingness to share our feelings and our vulnerability blocks relationships with both God and man. We
had to struggle with such questions as: Who is God as
I understand Him? What is His action in my life? Is my
understanding consistent with this action? What are my
feelings regarding Him, positive and negative? Who am
I in this relationship?

As recovery continued, we came to believe that our
very existence is a free gift from our Higher Power—
not as we once "understood Him," but as we have
come to understand Him through the awareness of His
action in our lives. When we are experiencing pain we
often need to look at the lives of others, particularly
those we sponsor, in order to see His action clearly.
Few of us would have survived our addiction without
God's aid.

We came to understand a God who is powerful, yet

gentle. We came to understand a God who loves us just
the way we are but too much to leave us that way. As our
conscious contact with God develops, it has the power to
transform our painful loneliness into joyful solitude.

It is through the Eleventh Step, the practice of prayer
and meditation, that we maintain and improve our conscious contact with God.

To do this we must come to that relationship anew
each day. We must be willing to let go of the old ideas
of who God was yesterday in terms of our understanding, and search continually for who He is in our lives
today. A conscious contact embraces not only the
known, but also acknowledges the mystery and the unknown as well. We also need to bring to prayer a conscious awareness of who we are by beginning an evening
session with "a constructive review of our day" as the
Big Book suggests.

The simplest way of describing the difference between prayer and meditation is that prayer is speaking
and meditation is listening. Any simple, spontaneous, honest sharing of who we are and how we feel
about the God of our understanding is prayer. Perhaps we are most familiar with prayer formulas like
The Lord's Prayer and The Serenity Prayer. Yet the
problem of unconsciousness can slip into these quite
easily. A helpful practice is to "journal" with our
favorite prayer formula from time to time—to sit down
and write the prayer out in our own words, or to go
through each phrase to discover what we mean by the
words we are saying. In using our daily meditation
books, we might read a passage to see what words
strike our hearts instead of reading with our intellect.
Do these words have something special to say to us
about our journey?

Meditation for most of us takes much practice, but it

is worth the effort. Being quiet, particularly in times of stress, is unfamiliar to most of us. Bill W. speaks often of "walking to serenity," and indeed a mile or so of walking can be meditation in itself as well as preparation for quiet time.

Finding a place with a comfortable chair and minimal stimulation is important. Many find soothing music aids in blocking out other internal and external distractions. Balancing the inhalation and exhalation of our breathing and gently, silently repeating a word such as "peace" or "love" are widely used techniques. For someone new to meditation, the *Twelve Steps and Twelve Traditions* offers some good suggestions in its discussion of the Eleventh Step. There are also many fine meditation guides available.

There are times when our attempts at prayer and meditation seem empty and unrewarding, and this can heighten our sense of loneliness. The "dark night" experience is common to all spiritual men and women. Someone described it as God's unwillingness to allow us to become addicted to Him, as surely we would if we received nothing but peak experiences. The low experiences give us the opportunity to develop our faith and trust that He is with us even when we are not directly aware of His presence. They also give us a greater appreciation for the gift of prayer when it does flow freely.

Perhaps the greatest barrier to the practice of the Eleventh Step is forgetting to pray and meditate. Another problem is that some of us have difficulty in disciplining ourselves to set aside the time required. We allow other areas of our lives to invade our prayer time. We are frequently shy about discussing our prayers with others and fear we're not doing it "right." Although we can always improve and expand our prayer and meditation, most of us quite naturally discover what works best for us. As our consciousness of God deepens, we receive the promised sense of belonging. We are never alone.

It is the tradition of Twelve Step recovery groups to share stories and make suggestions. It is hoped that these stories can be identified with and that some of the suggestions may be found helpful in seeking ways to deal with loneliness.

Loneliness is not an option. It may enter our lives for good reasons or for no reasons. So many of us are affected by it, yet we are often embarrassed to mention it. Perhaps we feel we should be doing better. The adage of ''pain shared is halved'' is true, but we sometimes forget. Keeping secrets prevents us from receiving the mixed blessing of loneliness: loneliness shared brings us into closer relationship with those with whom we share.

Pain acts as an effective catalyst for growth. It forces us to review and strengthen our recovery program. As is often said, ''The program is simple, not easy.'' Our experience is that walking through pain—with honesty, openness, and willingness—leads to new freedom and happiness.

May the loneliness you are now walking through bring you to greater awareness and acceptance of self, to deeper fellowship and intimacy with others, and to a growing experience of God's presence and love in your life.

REACHING
OUT TO
OTHERS

Each morning of the week, many members of Twelve Step groups regularly attend meetings at 7:00 A.M. called "Attitude Adjustment Hours."

These are people who understand the importance of reaching out, and they choose to begin their day this way. They recognize and act upon their need for fellowship, for moving out of isolation into areas of commonality and mutuality. They want to maintain and improve an exciting, satisfying way of life throughout the next 24 hours. Quite simply, they want to feel good and they know how to accomplish that without resorting to compulsive behaviors.

These members share an understanding of the importance of allowing other people into their lives. They know through experience that personal growth and recovery demand that we alter basic components in lifestyle. One of these is the need to extend ourselves to others.

No one who puts on a new pair of slippers needs to be told change is uncomfortable. The old pair of slippers, though tattered and threadbare, are friends, familiar and comfortable. The new ones feel stiff and awkward, and unless we throw away the old pair, there is always the temptation, especially when alone, to slip back into them.

This small, homely example of change can hardly be compared to the monumental challenge of recovery. But it does illustrate two important things: new behavior and attitudes are stiff and uncomfortable; and, it is easy to slip back into old ways, to regress, to relapse.

Loneliness, Isolation, and Boredom

The behavior of addicted people is stereotyped, repetitive, maladaptive, and rigid. Isolation is often entrenched and can be extremely subtle. We can be lonely in a room of three hundred people. We can live in a "loving" family and feel completely alone and unloved. The wonder is not that we have difficulty reaching out to others in recovery. The wonder is that we learn to do it at all!

It is a well-known fact we don't do what we *want* to do as much as those things we do by *habit*. Habits feel comfortable. Multiply this by about one million, and you have the dilemma of the learned, habitual response of addicts in avoiding life and self with alcohol, other drugs, sex, or food. What could possibly enable alcoholics and addicts and codependents to depart from such an ingrained lifestyle?

Addiction is the disease of loneliness, isolation, and boredom. Learning how to escape from such solitary confinement is a central lesson in recovery. Twelve Step groups undoubtedly attract the world's largest group of "loners" who discover their need and love for each other.

In addiction we pulled away, either actually or psychologically, from others. Instead of asking, "How are we alike?" we proclaimed "I'm special, unique, and different. You can't understand me, and I don't want to understand you. It's my life and I'll do with it as I please." Some of us had to die of our uniqueness. Others changed and live with varying degrees of joy and serenity.

In Twelve Step programs we become part of a great whole. It is an integrating way of life. We awake to the fact that even the Steps are written in the plural. They read *"We"* did these things. *"We"* came to understand. As the fog lifts, we realize that other people have been reaching out to us all along.

One day we actually *hear* and understand when someone says, "I can't. *We* can." What a powerful idea! Until this time our lives had been ruled by the idea that only people with mammoth amounts of willpower could achieve anything worthwhile in life. Our false pride, perfectionism, and delusion kept us from asking for any help.

Step One came as a bewilderment in its suggestion that our lives were beyond our management. We gradually began to see Steps Two and Three provided other management, something we could reach for if we became willing, honest, and open-minded.

An emphasis on surrender gradually permeated our self-centered, egotistical "Me First and Only" way of thinking and behaving. As we attended more meetings, not always understanding why we were there but feeling a glow and a lift by the meeting's end, we began doing something first *with* and then *for* others. What a switch! We cleaned ashtrays, made coffee, and stacked chairs. Our little jobs gave us a strange sense of satisfaction and usefulness, and the multilayered veneer of self-sufficiency and inflated ego began to crack. We started to enjoy the give and take of meetings. We even tried putting our trust in a Power greater than ourselves.

Dependence

The genius of Twelve Step programs directs dependence into constructive channels. Instead of "loving things and using people" the recovering person drops a self-destructive life-style and enters into interdependence with others. We begin using things and loving people. We switch our dependence to our Higher Power, and love working through the group. Each of us has the opportunity to offer and receive unconditional love with family, friends, and God.

The removal of drug use, overeating, or controlling others leaves a void. "The hole in my soul" is exposed. This enormous gap is filled to overflowing as we reach out to others and become involved. Older members suggest we select a sponsor, a mentor, a confidant, and as we grow older in the fellowship new members ask us to assume that role. We forge close, rich relations that last a lifetime. Loneliness, isolation, and boredom are strangers to us so long as we walk this path.

Working the Program

As ties of this kind develop we decide to do our best to live the Steps. When we hit a plateau, we may choose to complete another Fourth and then Fifth Step, reaching out again. We go from feeling egotistical and self-centered to realizing the truth of the prayer of St. Francis of Assisi, "It is in giving that we receive." As we extend love to others it comes back tenfold.

It is extremely difficult to go on hating and destroying yourself when you're doing something worthwhile for others or when you are active in sharing your strength, hope, and experience with the group. We raise our self-esteem in the lifelong process of pushing on to a higher level of maturity and adult responsibility. The rewards are magnificent.

Recovering people make restitution to their families, another dimension of reaching out. As loved ones experience their recoveries in Al-Anon, Nar-Anon, and O-Anon, all members learn to speak a common language. When we speak of miracles we include the wonder and blessing of reunited families. As C. S. Lewis wrote, "We should be ashamed of not performing miracles, and we do not feel this shame enough."

Staying close to our Twelve Step program helps us deal with perfectionism or defeatism. We don't have to accomplish the most, the best, the fastest. What you are is not what you do. Emphasis is on our spiritual way of life which allows us to live joyously and sanely "out there" in the great world as it exists. Twelve Step groups are filled with realism and pragmatism; "If it works, don't fix it." No one is expected to ascend to great heights or do outstanding deeds.

No Longer Alone

By freely reaching out we develop an accurate sense of significance. We gain perspective, and how important that is! We are no longer the center of the universe. Our preoccupation with self lessens as we tune in to the needs of others. Reciprocity replaces the obsession with our own misery. We become self-nurturing when we can say, "I have a God who loves me," and believe it.

We had reached a point at which we could no longer help ourselves, and it was only then that we became open to accepting assistance from others. We can't fully do this until we learn to trust. Trust is the magic balancing act in loving. Small children trust, and they are very open about wanting and enjoying friends. When we were caught up in addictive, compulsive behaviors, we removed ourselves from true camaraderie and stopped believing in friendship. We didn't trust anyone, including God, and we knew we couldn't trust ourselves.

It is inspiring to see what a big world of friends there is out there as we become interested in someone besides ourselves. We are no longer alone, and there is healing in this. Benjamin Franklin said, "When you are good to others you are best to yourself." We achieve self-acceptance and self-worth through acceptance of others. We attempt to extend nonconditional love to everyone, including ourselves.

The latter part is often the most difficult. The first commandment reads, "Love thy neighbor as *thyself*." Reaching out includes discovering our own authentic, genuine self. In being open to truly loving self and others, trust is essential. Most of the Twelve Step program, however, is based on trust and faith. As these grow we can offer each other a deeply personal gift: caring and sharing.

Communication is, of course, pivotal in this process. To live a spiritual way of life, we must express ourselves to others and actively listen to what they have to say. Many of us had to listen in the beginning to understand we were not completely insane. We were elated to learn any mental derangement might be temporary. Nowhere can we observe more interested or perceptive active listening than in Twelve Step meetings, and being heard today is a great luxury.

Many times we find we don't fully understand what we felt or thought until we hear someone reflect it to us. This accurate feedback holds a magnifying glass to our thoughts and impressions. We find special talents and abilities that enable us to truly *hear* each other, not only with our ears and minds, but with our hearts and sense of humor. It is important to be able to talk about the disease and be understood by those who have also experienced it.

Reaching Out

So much in recovery must be taken on faith. Becoming open-minded skeptics, we don't completely *know* why the Steps and the program work, but we see them working in the lives of others. The effects of the program shining in members and their families is palpable. If we but look and listen, we see and hear the pragmatic truth embodied in the lives of those we come to love. Whatever pit we are in when we enter recovery, we can see and hear someone who has climbed out of the same pit. That is part of the wonder of reaching out, of coming out of isolation, and we need only *be there* and employ our senses to acknowledge it.

We know, then, that many things serve together to encompass recovery, but if we stop and wonder whether or not the program is working in our lives we need only ask one question, Am I a joy to be with? If we are surly, supersensitive, or filled with resentments and self-pity, we may ask, When did I stop reaching out to give and receive help, compassion, and love? Rigorous honesty is a basis for trust, friendship, love, and service.

It doesn't matter in which direction we reach out first, vertically or horizontally. In either area we find self-transcendence. As we move closer to fellow Twelve Step members, we ignite love working through the group. Through the providence of our Twelve Step program we succeed, and we no longer need to bear the weighty burden of guilt. Forgiveness is a necessary blessing of the nonjudgmental program.

As we move through the accomplishment of Steps Eight and Nine we experience that, and we grow in perspective and humility so that we are able in Step Ten to "promptly admit" when we are wrong. In the all-encompassing petition of Step Eleven we see the ultimate direction for our attitudes, behaviors, and life's work. Then, when we are ready to acknowledge Step Twelve, we understand the true scope of reaching out.

None of this is automatic. We don't "do" the Steps once and then forget them. The sweep of the Twelve Step program requires eternal vigilance because of our vulnerabilities toward ego inflation, false pride, and the other nagging character defects and shortcomings.

The tug of our addiction or compulsion, our over-learned response to life, is strong and always there in the back of our minds. The urge to repeat these over-learned behaviors is perhaps the strongest pull we will ever know. And, we are not strong enough to secure a lasting victory in not doing it if we are left solely to our own devices.

Instead we establish the horizontal connection with others as we develop our vertical connection with a Power greater than ourselves. The Steps and other members guide us to this heightened spiritual dimension in life, and we may appreciate how subtly connected the horizontal and vertical planes are. In reaching out toward one, it is possible to enter both.

We may have felt foolish, terrified, or just plain bored with our youthful religious beliefs. We may have wanted to leave them behind forever. We may have been frightened, rebellious, or disinterested. We probably tried to bargain at times of desperation. The Twelve Steps afford us a more mature and loving approach to a Higher Power concept. We have a God who forgives and loves us.

We are only human, and falling into our old patterns of behavior is always a danger. Unless we guard carefully it will appear. We must go on reaching out. There is an inherent danger in accumulating many years of recovery without continually striving to improve its quality. Treatment centers, hospitals, and asylums are full of men and women who had achieved ten or more years of sobriety only to decide on a hot summer's day that they could ''handle a beer'' or a glass of wine with dinner. The road back to recovery is often long and arduous. There are those who never complete the journey.

In recovery we never reach the point at which we can coast. New members may not have the same problems we do, but working with them allows us to keep our memories fresh. This is ego deflation in action. Some people don't *want* to remember. That is dangerous. If nothing else, working with new members is cheap insurance against relapse. To the truly dedicated, it is much more.

A.A. emerged as the outstanding self-help movement of this century in the 1930s because one man knew he desperately needed to change. He reached out to another alcoholic, who happened to be a physician. These men had many question marks in their early working format for sobriety, but they recognized from the very beginnings of this powerful fellowship the importance of extending self to others. Soon thereafter, numerous Twelve Step groups (Narcotics Anonymous, Overeaters Anonymous, Codependents Anonymous) were formed, based on A.A.'s Twelve Steps.

When we come into a Twelve Step program today we may feel sentenced to a life of bread and water. The "good old days" have vanished never to return, and we mourn their loss. As we begin to relish the feast of life the program provides, we give ourselves permission to change and become as fully human as possible. We savor the true, deep flavors of recovery, and we learn to laugh at "the bad old days." At first, we grudgingly allow ourselves to receive from others in the fellowship. Then we gradually continue that legacy by giving to those who follow. We give as it was given to us. We find self-worth, self-acceptance, and legitimate self-esteem by passing on the gift.

Reaching out can't end at five or ten or twenty years or any other length of time if we wish to continue the miracle of our rebirth. We nurture others and are fed in return, or we wither. In taking the risk of reaching out, we form truly intimate relationships. Fellowship delivers us from the tyranny of addictions and compulsions, and the power struggle ends. We let go and let God. We develop the ability to care, to love, and to give. We become playful and alive.

LIVING
THE
PRINCIPLES

ALCOHOLICS ANONYMOUS, THE BIG BOOK, TELLS US on page 60, "No one among us has been able to maintain anything like perfect adherence to these principles. We are not saints. The point is, that we are willing to grow along spiritual lines. The principles we have set down are guides to progress. We claim spiritual progress rather than spiritual perfection."

Some of us should be excused for the vast relief we felt when we first read this statement in the Big Book. After all, it follows the Twelve Steps, which can sound very righteous to a person just coming off a drunk. "It was great to learn that I didn't have to become a holier-than-thou in order to stay sober," is a typical reaction. "I wanted to get well by tomorrow, but I was willing to wait until next week for sainthood!"

Although we won't become saints, the Twelve Step program does give us principles that bring dramatic change in our lives. Even without "perfect adherence," every person who is really successful in recovery follows a few key principles with deep conviction and great understanding. How does this happen, and how *do* we go about living the Twelve Step principles?

Judging from what we hear at meetings, living a Twelve Step program is not always a smooth process for some of us, nor do we approach it with the same gusto we once displayed toward drinking, using other drugs, gambling, or overeating. "I looked at the principles very suspiciously and resentfully," a member recalls. "It was only after I suffered a lot more and made additional mistakes that I became really willing to give the Steps a chance. And it was a long time before I could really appreciate the full value and depth of this program."

In other words, the Twelve Step principles only become important to us after we realize we need them, and often the need has to be desperate. We live or practice our principles if we really feel it's required for our recovery and self-improvement. This may seem selfish to some, but it is also positive and realistic. Outsiders sometimes resent it when Twelve Step group members declare, "This is a selfish program." But those selfish reasons also ensure that we will try to practice a principle when we really value and understand it.

First We Surrender

It is difficult to rank the various principles of Twelve Step programs according to importance. Very little ever happens, however, until the individual surrenders the problem. In the *Twelve Steps and Twelve Traditions*, Bill W. notes on pages 21 and 22: "The principle that we shall find no enduring strength until we first admit complete defeat is the main taproot from which our whole Society has sprung and flowered."

Admitting complete defeat is a very high hurdle for victims of addictions and compulsions. Since we can easily deceive ourselves about our true motives, the safest approach is to think of surrender as something that should be affirmed frequently. Many recovering people think of a slip as something that starts occurring long before the person actually slips. "What really slipped was my thinking," a returning person will say. "I started to look at the bright lights and to think something exciting was going on in my old haunts. Pretty soon I stopped remembering how bad it had been. Before long, I was back to my old ways."

When a slip occurs, we can ask ourselves: Did it happen because we withdrew our earlier surrender, or was our surrender never truly complete in the first place? All we need to know is, the compulsion to act out certain behaviors is so powerful and persistent that the price of freedom is constant vigilance. The stakes are so high that Twelve Step members make it a principle never to do anything that might put their recovery at risk. Perhaps for this reason, the surrender principle has sired a number of sayings which are often heard at meetings. "Stay off the Slippery Slopes," "Keep it Simple," "One Day at a Time" are sayings which help make this principle an enduring part of our lives.

Let Go and Let God

Another great principle of Twelve Step programs is surrender to a Higher Power or "Let Go and Let God." Each person finds his or her own effective way to benefit from it. This was something the pioneering A.A. members discovered through trial and error in their early years of struggle. It was known, for example, that profound religious or spiritual experiences had enabled some people to recover from alcoholism. But because of such things as temperament and childhood experiences, many of us found it impossible to accept such beliefs, even while knowing we desperately needed the help it might bring.

We should always be grateful to those who discovered it wasn't necessary to accept another's concept of God in order to make conscious contact with a Higher Power. "That was great news to us," the Big Book says on page 47, "for we had assumed we could not make use of spiritual principles unless we accepted many things on faith which seemed difficult to believe." The Big Book authors discovered that the "Realm of Spirit," as they called it, is broad, roomy, all inclusive, and open to all who seek it.

As recovering people, how do we find this Realm of Spirit in our lives? This is an intensely personal matter. Some people combine this searching with formal religious activity; others say they have no need for this. A few say they must pray on their knees, while others say they have beautiful spiritual contacts as they go about their daily work. The guideline for progress seems to be, whatever works for you and brings lasting benefit must be your right way.

Some people insist we should not expect guidance from our Higher Power on personal matters like job changes, marriage plans, financial troubles, and purchase decisions. But how can they say that these are *not* proper matters for prayer and meditation? We can easily make serious mistakes in any of these areas that will threaten our happiness and well-being. If we truly practice sound principles in *all* our affairs, this may include seeking guidance from our Higher Power for any decision that concerns us. Members frequently say, however, that they have little success with "gimme" prayers. But they often do fairly well when they are able to "turn things over" without trying to dictate the outcome. And the reason may be that we often do not really know which answer will bring us the most good or benefit.

See God in the Situation

Emmet Fox, whose writings were immensely important to the first Twelve Step members, said we can bring our Higher Power into any negotiation by seeing God on both sides of the table. "Claim that God is working through both of you, through yourself and through the person with whom you are dealing," Fox wrote in *Power Through Constructive Thinking*. "Do not seek by will power to get your own way, but affirm that God's will in that particular matter is being done. Remember that your own way may not be at all good for you. The very thing that you want today may turn out next week to be a nuisance or even a misfortune."

Fox went on to say that by seeing "God on both sides" of a negotiation, the outcome will always be successful for both parties. This will be true even if we do not get the arrangement we sought at the outset; a better one would appear shortly.

One person had startling proof that this principle works. He wanted to purchase a small business. He had even been praying for guidance in the matter. Just as he was about to close the deal, it fell through and he became terribly discouraged. Other members reminded him the disappointment could be the hand of God working in a mysterious way, and God never closes one door without causing another to open. He was urged to believe that God was in charge of the situation.

He admitted that he found these statements annoying, but at the same time they were comforting. Impatience—"we want what we want, and we want it now"—is a false principle that can lead to serious blunders. But he accepted the disappointment and after a few days even began to believe the business disappointment may have been for his good.

It worked out beautifully. Within weeks another business opportunity appeared, and he moved easily into it. It was a much better situation than the first. He also realized that if the original deal had gone through, he wouldn't have been in the position to take advantage of the better opportunity.

This kind of experience, which happens in many people's lives, suggests that a Higher Power is working on our behalf. Sometimes the results appear to be coincidental, but many people who experience spiritual guidance insist they don't believe in coincidence. As one person puts it, "Coincidence is when God sends a beautiful message without signing His name!"

Walk the Walk

Although they are far from saintlike, most solid members in Twelve Step programs will agree that success in recovery includes the effort to live up to high standards in their lives. It is very damaging in recovery, for example, to be viewed as someone who "talks the talk" but does not "walk the walk." Since recovering people are not expected to be saints, what are the minimum standards that are considered in living the program?

Most of the time, honesty and fairness seem to be expected of people in Twelve Step programs. At one meeting, a young member confessed to shoplifting even though he had been abstinent for quite some time. While shoplifting had been accepted in his old peer group, there was a general agreement at the A.A. table that shoplifting violates the principles of the program; it is indefensibly wrong.

At the same time, other members seemed to understand the pressures and desires that may have led to the crime. Some members admitted dishonesties of their own, while others offered constructive opinions. The entire discussion actually ended on a high note by underscoring the importance of positive actions.

Sometimes we can benefit from following principles which appear to have no direct bearing on a problem we are faced with, yet these principles can make us feel better about ourselves. Here is an example:

A member was driving to an important anniversary meeting where he was the guest speaker. He was on an interstate highway and still 50 miles from his destination, when he passed a woman and her two children stranded in their disabled automobile.

An inner voice told him he should turn back to help. Another voice argued he was almost late for the meeting, the state patrol would probably arrive any minute to help, or some other motorist would stop.

But he turned back at the next exit. Experience had taught him he wouldn't feel right about himself if he ignored the first voice.

His assistance to the stranded family delayed him only fifteen minutes, and he arrived just as the meeting was starting. His talk went especially well—the result, he believed, of following the right principle in responding to the family on the highway.

Sharing is another basic principle of every Twelve Step program, although it can be expressed in many forms. A member in Nebraska has an unusual way of practicing sharing principles in his hobby of candy making. He has been making candy for ten years and says, "I try to be a little better each time." He distributes hundreds of pieces of candy each week to the local treatment center, to nurses at the hospital, and to residents of a senior citizen home. He also mails boxes of candy to friends.

"I have one principle connected with this hobby," he says. "I never sell any candy. I have a few principles like this that I use for practice, so that I can become adept at 'practicing these principles in all my affairs.' "

There is certainly nothing wrong with selling candy, as this man did years ago when he operated a grocery store. Today, however, making and freely sharing his candy adds something special to his long years of recovery.

Using Principles at Work

Many people in recovery programs suffer from feelings of fear and inadequacy at work. An early member, who felt threatened by pressures and problems on the job, used a program slogan to meet the challenge.

His job was to regulate traffic flow from a small tower over a busy railroad intersection. Automobile traffic sometimes became jammed in all four directions while express trains pounded in on crisscrossing tracks. He had scary moments when collisions seemed imminent.

But he had a simple plan for handling traffic jams at the crossing. First, he would stop traffic in all directions. Then he would study the situation, without letting himself be intimidated by horn blasts from angry motorists. Finally he would let the trains pass; then he would release each line of traffic until the crossing was cleared. It always worked for him.

"I just think about the slogan 'First Things First,' " he says. "It's a piece of the program you can apply to your work or anything you do."

We Are Guided to Action

"Guides to progress" is a fitting way to describe the Twelve Steps. These principles are generally defined as "fundamental guides to action." For most of us, the action must lead to progress in the form of recovering sanity, living at peace with the world, developing our own talents and abilities, and taking responsibility for our own lives. "Growing along spiritual lines" is another way of saying our principles come from God and are part of the universal system. As one spiritual teacher says, "We do not create laws and principles but discover and make use of them."

For most of us, continued success in overcoming our major problems proves we are living our principles. We should also notice progress in other areas: more happiness, better relations with others, improved self-understanding, and growth in maturity—all of these can happen in the program. If we are on the path and moving forward, we are doing well.

When our progress seems to be temporarily delayed, we can remember we are not expected to become saints by next week. Even the saints had to wait centuries for their sainthood!

INADEQUACY

THOUGHTS, FEELINGS, AND FEARS ABOUT INADE-
quacy present a paradox of special importance to recovering people. In order to achieve emotional growth
we must learn to distinguish between those feelings of
inadequacy which cripple us and those which are
healthy, normal, and essential to growth.

The Malady of Measurement

Everywhere we go we are measured. We are either
short or tall, rich or poor, fat or thin, smart or dumb.
And the actual numbers really don't matter—being six
feet tall may make one a foot too short for professional
basketball and way oversized to be a jockey.

In addition to the numbers we can see, it seems as if
everything about us has some place on another yard-
stick, an invisible scale which reads INADEQUACY at
the low end and COMPETENCE at its top. With competence comes the glow of pride, while inadequacy is
almost a synonym for embarrassment. If it is important

to us to be thin, then our ability to lose weight makes us proud. If we feel too "little" to be counted as a "full-sized" person, then we may be embarrassed to feel thin. People will work very hard to achieve pride and avoid the label of inadequacy.

Whenever we feel inadequate, the mind gives us an instant "readout" of what might have caused it. Even if the moment of embarrassment is healthy, as when we face up to the fact that the power of our Higher Power is much greater than our own, such understanding is difficult for us. Any moment of inadequacy produces *thoughts* of all such experiences—being little, dirty, incompetent, helpless, weak, a fake, or phony. We all protect ourselves against embarrassment in ways which are colored by our experiences.

Sometimes it doesn't matter who is doing the measuring. We can judge ourselves more harshly than anybody else might, or we can excuse ourselves to avoid self-judgment. One of the wonderful things about the fellowship of a Twelve Step program is that by joining, a member accepts the identity, "I am an alcoholic," or "I am an overeater," and no longer needs to worry about the self-judgment which usually accompanies that particular label. The more deeply involved we are in our addictive behavior the more difficult it becomes to judge ourselves accurately.

A related paradox is the observation that when we feel the most inadequate and the least able to face our friends, this is precisely the time we would benefit most from meeting them.

Self-Esteem

So, why do we measure so much? Most likely it is simply because we find it easier to point to a number than to a feeling. It is easier to say, "I can drink a quart of beer 3.3 seconds faster than anybody else in the world," than it is to say, "I feel good about myself today." Self-esteem is fragile, based on flimsy evidence, and always under attack. In the healthiest and most successful among us it seems to derive from the certainty that one has lived up to some sort of goal.

This is not the kind of goal children set when they want to grow up to be cowboys, race car drivers, or movie stars. Those are better understood as fantasies in which a child wants to take on the entire identity of the admired person. Cartoon characters like Superman are wonderful for both children and adults because they are so perfect, so invulnerable that we can never really expect to be like them—we know instinctively that everybody is inadequate compared to them. When we fantasize we are Superman (a healthy use of fantasy), we are taking on a temporary identity which wipes away our inadequacy for a moment and lets us return to our real selves in a better mood. When we need external substances to make the fantasy more "real" we are losing reasonable control of our senses.

The more mature we are and the more we have learned the lessons of the Twelve Steps, the more our self-esteem is based on attainable goals. Psychotherapists have often observed that people who are getting well in any treatment program begin to take on some sort of physical discipline, like jogging or calisthenics. They have discovered it feels wonderful to set a goal and make it.

Then What Are Emotions?

It is vital for us to understand that emotions do not mean anything specific at all. There can never by any "basic" or "true" meaning of embarrassment, guilt, anger, anxiety, or excitement. These emotions are part of a biological sensory system which protects us much like the more conventional senses of sight, hearing, smell, taste, touch, as well as temperature, pain, and balance. Just as pain teaches the lion to look at a paw and remove the offending thorn, and smell asks us to glance inquisitively toward the kitchen, the feeling of inadequacy asks that we search within ourselves to see what truth has been exposed and why we needed to hide it, as well as hide from it.

The Twelve Steps

Examine the Twelve Steps of Alcoholics Anonymous for a moment. In order to admit we are *powerless* over alcohol (or other drugs, gambling, sex, overeating), we must be able to accept that, relative to our problem behavior, we are inadequate. This *healthy* feeling is of critical importance—it is necessary for the beginning of true emotional growth. Thus, Step One demands acceptance of inadequacy, as does Step Two, in which we come to understand not only that evil can be more powerful than ourselves, but that the forces of good can be even more powerful. We experience healthy inadequacy from the fact that *both* forces are more powerful than our own!

Early, Halting Steps

Let us look through the rest of the Twelve Steps and ask ourselves whether the shame and guilt they produce have anything to do with the difficulty they present us. Step Three asks us to turn ourselves over to the care of God, thus requiring even further acceptance of our inadequacy relative to this Higher Power. In doing this we become passive, which at one time might have made us feel ashamed. It is a delusion to think we are competent to run our own lives when we are really the victims of our addiction or compulsion.

Unless we accept that God's Power is loving and benign, that it represents true safety and security, as opposed to the false security of our addiction or compulsion, we cannot in good conscience go to Step Four—which requires the kind of fearless moral inventory which might be emotionally devastating had we not the power and love of God behind us. Naturally, you can see that what we fear from such a searching look at what we have been trying to hide is awareness of our own shortcomings and thus a terrifying dose of inadequacy.

Getting There

Step Five asks us to admit we have done wrong, which means we accept guilt—but it also requires us to admit this guilt to God, to ourselves, and to another human being. This exposure must carry with it some experience of shame, despite the fact that the more love there is in our lives, the less we need to fear feeling inadequate.

In Step Six we must once again recognize we are

helpless, woefully inadequate to change ourselves, and that only God can change us. Were we falsely perfectionistic, self-proud, or egotistical, it is at this point that we might never be able to accept that to have defects is human, while it is in the province of God to remove them so we may live as whole people. And in Step Seven we march that extra mile and actually ask, with true humility, that God remove these reasons for our inadequacy.

Many people think of alcohol, other drugs, food, or certain behaviors as pain killers. It works pretty well for shame, too. Until we are willing to accept our inadequacy, and all the pain which accompanies it, we are not likely to have a strong recovery. Everyone who has achieved recovery knows the familiar sting of embarrassment which accompanies recognition of our inadequacy. Only those who are stuck in bravado, in machismo, and in other forms of falsely elevated self-esteem, can claim that they are unaffected by inadequacy.

Strong, Firm Steps

In Step Eight we must look into the past and face ourselves as we have been. What pain must afflict us as we realize what we did to those closest to us, and even to those who never mattered to us before! The pain which greets our recognition of the harm we did others is guilt, while the combination of guilt and humiliation makes it difficult for us to think about making amends to our victims. Small wonder that many of us find the frail craft of our recovery floundering on the shoals of Step Eight!

But if we persevere, Step Nine is ours, and we can

make direct amends, unless, of course, doing so would embarrass those we wish to help. It would be terrible selfishness on our part to sacrifice the calm of another merely to reduce our guilt. Step Nine requires great heart, delicacy, and tact. Tact implies awareness of how the other person feels about his or her inadequacy.

The Final Steps

The last three Steps are just as demanding as the preceding nine, for they require perpetual vigilance and perpetual willingness to experience inadequacy and guilt. In Step Ten we make a thorough commitment to inner openness, to a life in which we accept the shame of seeing whatever shortcomings may appear in our constant personal inventory. It is something like the farmer who clears the rocks from his field year after year, wondering whether he will ever see a spring with his fields free of new rocks. Yet it is these same field-stones which become the walls of his house and his lands—what turns up in our ongoing personal inventory becomes the material from which we rebuild ourselves continually. Inadequacy must be faced and accepted; what produces guilt must be admitted and repaired.

In the egotism of our addiction or compulsion we tried to hide our inadequacy and preferred to claim (defective though we are) that we were masters of our own lives rather than the instruments of God. Prayer is nothing more than a conversation with God as we understand Him, while meditation is a conversation within ourselves couched in what we feel is a language acceptable to God. In Step Eleven we pray for knowledge of His will for us, and that we be granted the Power to carry out that will. Only when we have accepted our personal inadequacy and given up our fantasy of personal perfection can we approach the degree of enlightenment needed to become a clear vehicle for the expression of God's will.

Finally, Step Twelve takes for granted that we have realized this spiritual awakening which is the goal of all followers of the Twelve Step path toward wholeness. Further, it asks that we can now find within ourselves the willingness and strength to go out into the world and, from our own example, teach others what we have learned. In order to do this, we must live each and every principle in every moment of our lives—accepting inadequacy when we find another stone in our field, and guilt when we admit we have used that stone to harm another. Wholeness demands such acceptance of self.

The Shame Weapon

There is an intimate relationship between pride, love and self-esteem—anything which affects one will affect the others. We cheer the victors in a contest and hoist them on our shoulders to show our love for them. Whenever we suffer a defeat, with all its potential for the loss of self-esteem, we experience both inadequacy and shame, making us feel unlovable. Everybody knows false flattery should be avoided—we are vulnerable to those who manipulate us by the shoddy trick of making us feel loved so we will treat them better. What is not as well recognized is that it is just as cruel to manipulate people by unleashing the shame weapon.

Those who love us, or those to whom we are important, look to us for confirmation of their self-esteem. Generally, when we are in a good mood, we are happy to make those around us happy. But when we are in a bad mood, or when we have suffered a defeat in the game of life and are in the shadow of an inadequacy we cannot bear to face, it is more difficult for us to make anybody happy.

At such moments, having just failed, we may doubt our ability to ever succeed again and we may not be able to raise our self-esteem. The moment of inadequacy has reduced us relative to those around us. In reaction, we tend to lash out at others, especially those closest to us and most dependent on us, in order to reduce their self-esteem so that we do not feel a gulf between us and them. In this sense, making somebody miserable gives us a rush of power, which begins to undo our feeling of inadequacy. It is unfortunate that we use the shame weapon.

In arguments, people tend to accuse each other of having *done* something awful, which produces the emotion guilt, or they brand the other as *being* something awful, thus producing the kind of embarrassment which makes us feel inadequate. The accused can usually deny the guilt, but can only escape the feeling of inadequacy by causing an equal amount of shame in the other. Thus, family arguments usually result in the loser hiding, whether in the privacy of one's room, by ''going home to mother,'' or by drowning inadequacy in drink, food, drugs, or sex.

Interviews with adult children of unhealthy families reveal such families have an increased tendency to use embarrassment as the most prominent weapon. Children of abusive parents almost universally shudder when they talk about the ways their parents shamed them. Frequently they describe the terrible sense of inadequacy which haunted them, for it is largely from our parents that we derive our sense of self.

The Reawakened Self

It is only through the lessons of the Twelve Steps that we can learn to face ourselves, to deal with the guilt we feel for what we have done to others, and to recognize our natural and human inadequacies. The more we study and learn, the more there is to learn. This work on ourselves is life-long, as it is for all people. Sometimes it may seem an unbearable experience to deal with the reawakened sense of inadequacy and guilt which accompany our journey towards wholeness. No book can cure, no tract can treat. Perhaps you will read this book many times over, referring to it time and again as you find within yourself questions about the pain of inadequacy, sharing with others passages you have found personally helpful.

And we must never lose sight of the guiding principles which have made the Twelve Steps such a powerful force for good. It is through our association with others that we have gained the strength to recover. This relationship to the group is essential for true recovery, for we live *in* the world, not remote and isolated from it. The Twelve Step program provides a model for the world as it can be, a world of fellowship—not a fellowship of perfect people, all free of blemish, but a fellowship of people with the wonderful variety that makes us truly human. It is not that we are inadequate compared to others, not that we are superior or inferior, but that we are human.

HOPE

THERE IS AN OLD MEXICAN STORY THAT ILLUSTRATES the importance of hope for a full and healthy life. The story says one day the devil decided to go out of business. He held an auction to dispose of all the instruments of temptation he had used. Many people attended this auction hoping to find a means to achieve their wants through one of these instruments. The auction began early in the day, but there was not as much interest as one would expect. In fact, people were surprised to see most of the tools shiny and new, as though they had never been used.

The bidding was slow and most of the instruments were sold at a low price. Toward evening, there was only one left. It differed from the others in that it was well worn, so the bidding began high and continued even higher. Some people asked the devil's assistants what this instrument was that commanded such a high price. The assistants said it was a tool of the devil used most frequently and found most useful. It was the temptation to despair. They explained that the devil found, once he could get people to give up hope, the rest was easy.

Many of us who are recovering can recall times when we lived without hope. It was lack of hope that produced the familiar sense of impending doom. Even when we hid our despair and fear of the future behind a mask of bravery, it seemed as though we were caught in a situation that could only get worse. We may have contemplated suicide as a way out of the situation. Being without hope, we had no real sense that the future could be anything different from the present.

Experience + Strength = Hope

A Twelve Step meeting is a fellowship in which people share their experience, strength, and hope. In fact, experience, strength, and hope are interrelated. The open sharing of our experience of recovery is the source of our strength. The willingness to share what has worked for us, the mistakes we've made and survived, the difficulties we have overcome, our willingness to accept care from others in recovery, all contribute to a strength that no one of us has on our own. It would seem that this willingness to share is not an option for us. And sharing experience is not limited to swapping "war stories" of addictive behaviors. We need to share the experience of today if we are to find strength to live it.

It is shared experience plus strength that flows from sharing and that becomes the foundation for hope. Hope is personal, but never individualistic. Hope is a shared reality or it is not real at all. This may seem to be an extreme statement, but upon examination it appears to be true. It is most obvious in the case of recovery. Many of us have tried to go it alone, to do it our way, and then discovered we could not. The attempt to live for ourselves, by ourselves, inevitably ends in frustration and despair. It was only when we began to share our experience that we gained strength and could begin to hope.

This simple lesson we first learned in terms of recovery is sometimes difficult to apply in other areas of our lives. Even after years of recovery we may sense a lack of fullness in our lives that we see in others around us. We may discover we have a lack of hope for the future. Routine, a lack of zest in living, even a sense of cynicism, may creep back into our daily lives.

The future may hold no promise for us other than a confused sense of "getting through." This lack of hope for the future and our lives may be related to our willingness to share experience and strength. We not only need to be willing to give, but also to be open to receiving from others. One of the things that can happen is we may have become givers and not receivers. Hope can be revitalized by a willingness to accept help from others; to allow our lives to be touched and influenced by others' experience and strength.

Hope versus Fantasy

We may have spent a lot of time in magical or wishful thinking when we were suffering from our illness—whether it was chemical dependency, overeating, or codependency. We may have fantasized about winning the lottery, getting a big promotion, or finding just the right person who would make life worthwhile. Our addiction or compulsion encouraged us to live in fantasy rather than reality.

The difference between fantasizing and hoping is in their relationship to the present. Fantasy bears no relationship to the present in any real way. It is simply a new world created by our wishes and desires, without any steps to get from here to there. True, some of us do win lotteries, or we get an unexpected promotion, or we meet someone special that makes a real difference in our lives. But we have to at least make the effort of buying the ticket, or doing the work, or getting out and meeting people.

Hope and Simplicity

One of the major blocks to hope is our tendency to complicate a situation. Give most of us five minutes alone with a simple problem and we can create a maze that defies imagination. This tendency was prevalent before recovery began, but our capacity for complication continues well into recovery.

Albert Einstein developed great mathematical theories long before the days of computers. However, he was given a special room comprised almost entirely of blackboards on which to do his complicated math. Every day when he left, he would leave a note on each blackboard that said either "erase" or "do not erase." One day the blackboard cleaner came into the room and saw that on each blackboard Einstein had written "erase" except in one small corner. Here he marked off a square in which he wrote a famous formula, and under that he wrote "do not erase." The formula was $2 + 2 = 4$. Einstein, with his great mathematical mind could range into the complicated far beyond the capacity of most people. He not only had a sense of humor, but a grasp of the importance of basics.

Simplicity of life is not being simpleminded. Some of us may have a natural predisposition toward a more ordered and simple life-style than others. All of us tend, however, to let our lives become unnecessarily cluttered. The clutter becomes a real block to active hope because we find ourselves, unaware at times, in the midst of contradictions.

An example of contradiction might be when we wanted to drink or use and yet still stay sober and not cause trouble. Contradictions lead us to create conflicts in ourselves because we are charging into reality and attempting to mold it to our desires. When we keep hope simple and direct, we can conform to reality and our hope has a much greater chance of surviving.

Sometimes we need to share our hopes to see if they are contradictory. If they are, we need to let go of one desire in favor of another, or place it on hold for a while. For example, someone may wish to complete training for a new career, develop some hobbies, and pursue a relationship. These need not be in conflict, but they may be. It might be necessary to give priority to one over the other. In each instance, however, we need to keep in line with the basic hope of abstinent living. If taking steps to fulfill some of our hopes would conflict with our basic program, then we could cause problems. Keeping it simple in this case means sharing hopes with others so that we keep them from being in conflict and keep our recovery in proper perspective.

Hope and Patience

For most of us, patience has not been one of our strong suits. If anything, we have tended to be people who want it all, now. To hope is not to demand. Some of us know ourselves well enough to realize we often overreact in response to our thoughts or desires. To learn hope is to learn patience. Again, shared experience and strength of many recovering people have taught us that even our wildest hopes can be fulfilled, but not necessarily on our time schedule. Impatience can be an enemy of hope. We may know from experience that impatience has sometimes ruined a relationship or a job. We may have acted too quickly, without consultation or prayer, and ruined a friendship. We can learn from our mistakes of impatience the value of taking time. In fact, patience is not simply waiting and watching the grass grow. Patience is waiting with hope.

Again, it is helpful to share with another the difficulty of waiting and to acknowledge our tendency toward impatience. By sharing, we develop hope and avoid some of the dangers that occur when we become too demanding. There is no neat formula for all of this. The art of living with hope is acquired through practice and that means we all make mistakes. But there is hope even in that, for we can learn to develop a sense of personal timing, regarding when to act and when to wait.

Hope and the Pain of Loss and Failure

At first, recovery may seem to promise that all trials are behind us. The gift of recovery appears to bring with it all the things we wanted. Not everyone has this pink cloud experience early in recovery. But during the first few years, there are not many of us who don't, at some time, have the feeling that we may have "turned the corner." We begin to suspect that life is going to unfold smoothly for us. However, after some time in recovery, all of us come to the realization that although recovery is our greatest gift and the promises of the program are true, we continue to face the reality of the pain of loss and failure in our lives.

These times are very important for us. We learn that hope is not simply an optimism that denies the pain of living. We learn, too, that our recovery is not fragile. Recovery does not depend on things going our way. It does not rest on a foundation of continued success. We discover that hope is not grounded in ourselves, but rather in a Power greater than ourselves that we allow to work in our lives. It is in times of distress that we come to a deeper realization of our need for others to support our hope for life. Hope does not blithely turn away from pain. Rather it enables us to face the pain of loss or failure.

Among the more severe pains we may face is the loss of a loved one through death or the loss of a relationship through divorce or separation. It is important for us to be aware that the pain of such losses is not incompatible with hope. The pain is real and we need to grieve the loss. A great deal has been written about the phenomenon of grief. Grieving over real losses in our lives is a complex process accompanied by many intense feelings. Sometimes we may experience a very real sense of guilt. We may have sudden rushes of anger toward the other person, or God, or ourselves. We may wonder why such a loss should happen to us. We may at times wonder if having worked so hard was worth it.

Hope plays two important functions in such times of loss. If we understand hope to be *the confident expectation of good*, it enables us to go through the grieving process abstinent and come to a full acceptance of our loss. Hope reminds us that although the loss of a loved one through death or separation will indeed affect our lives, the intensity of the emotion will pass. Hope encourages us to reach out to others for help. Hope gives us the strength to accept our feelings realizing that no matter how powerful they may be, they do not have the power to destroy us.

Hope also enables us to see the importance of mourning and coming to a full acceptance of the loss in order that hope may flourish again. If we attempt to bypass this grieving process by pretending nothing has happened, or if we allow ourselves to become caught in the anger which may accompany grief, we short-circuit our capacity for genuine hope for the future.

To grieve the loss of a friend or loved one is not at all contrary to hope. If a person has truly been a gift in our lives and we experience the loss of that person, a certain sadness is bound to follow. But mourning loss need not go on forever. As we grieve the loss and come to the full acceptance of it, another future begins to emerge. It is hope that allows us to look forward in life with a calm and confident expectation of good.

The pains of loss and of failure are frequently interrelated and difficult to distinguish. However, we can separate them. Frequently, a loss is not our responsibility. Failure seems to imply a sense of, "It could have been different if only I had. . . ." In ongoing recovery, we continue to learn to deal with failure in a healthy and hopeful way. Perhaps what hope teaches us in regard to failure is that no failure is final until we resolve it. The pain of not achieving a cherished goal may be real. Hope, however, allows us to acknowledge we have failed and helps us realize that it does not mean we are failures. In this instance hope enables us to look for the good in the experience and in ourselves. Hope encourages us to acknowledge, but not dwell on the past.

Many of us have gone through very significant losses and failures in our addictive and compulsive careers. In recovery we have learned to look back on those and see that they need not inflict permanent damage on our lives. In recovery, as we face the reality of the pain of loss and failure, we realize we have resources to draw upon through the program and the people in it that we never had before. Hope does not do away with pain, but allows us to accept it and live with a certain grace.

Hope as a Way of Life

Hope is a way of envisioning the future. It implies not only the wish that things will be different, but a willingness to change and the courage to act. Hopes tell us a great deal about ourselves. They reveal what is deep in our hearts and minds. In recovery we discover we have hope not only for ourselves but for other recovering people, our families, even our careers. Hope leads us out of ourselves, helps us become less self-centered, and be more concerned for the welfare of others.

Hope can see us through difficult and painful situations, and provide meaning and purpose. When things go well and hope has been fulfilled, we have an opportunity for gratitude, and we can look forward to an even happier future.

Developing Hope

There are several small things we can do to help develop our capacity for hope. We might, for example, write down our hopes and specific goals on a regular basis and share them with others. We could call this taking an inventory of the future, rather than of the past.

It will reveal the difference between what we truly hope for and what we fantasize about.

Another means of developing our capacity for hope involves Step Eleven, which asks us to improve our conscious contact with God *as we understand Him*, praying for knowledge of His will for us and the power to carry that out. As we learn to take time for prayer and meditation, we discover new possibilities we never considered. If we are willing to take our hope to our Higher Power in prayer and meditation, our hope will be expanded, and we will come to a deeper realization that fulfillment of hope does not depend on us alone.

If we are willing to share experience and strength, hope can become a way of life. We no longer have to regret the past, because we are learning how to look with confidence to the future. The openness with which we are willing to accept our past may be the only barrier to hope. As we grow in honesty, openness, and willingness, we realize our hope will not be in vain. Willingness to examine and share our hopes, to be patient and keep it simple, to take time for prayer and meditation, become the foundation for a life today which looks forward to the future with the *confident expectation of good*.

LOVING
RELATIONSHIPS

In the past, we had our loving relationships with our addictive substance or thoughts rather than with people. We became increasingly isolated from those around us. We may have attempted to reach out to others, but our efforts were unsuccessful because we didn't understand what had happened to us. When we initiate a recovery program, we learn we are not alone and there are many others who have struggled as we have. We learn we *can* change, and we see loving relationships are a possibility and, in fact, a necessity. We are all capable of having loving relationships!

Loving Relationships Bloom Over Time

A loving relationship is not an entity to be possessed. Loving relationships evolve, just as individuals change from day to day and develop into new and healthier people. Relationships are a process; they are not static. Like a rose unfolding, a relationship should be enjoyed and treasured through each stage of blossoming.

To begin a loving relationship, we must be open, trusting ourselves and others. Trust and openness depend on each other in loving relationships and, for most of us, require courage. The Serenity Prayer has helped many of us find the courage within to risk trust and openness.

Twelve Step programs emphasize the necessity of acceptance of ourselves and our imperfections, and acceptance of others and their imperfections. This quality gives us the flexibility to be gentle with ourselves and to interact with others in a healthy manner.

As we grew up, we developed many beliefs about relationships and how they should be conducted. As a result of these beliefs, we created many painful relationships. We then blamed ourselves and those we were involved with. This created further pain. The only way out is when we begin to see that we must challenge our old beliefs in order to experience fulfilling and joyful relationships. Some of these beliefs may include perceptions about traditional role models for men and women. They also include stereotypes of how women and men express their feelings, such as "hysterical women" or "macho men." Society seems to demand that we be in relationships, and that ideally, these relationships should culminate in marriage and children. If we find ourselves living in ways that don't match these beliefs, we may be filled with negative feelings about ourselves and society.

We have been living in such a way that we have given power to a variety of external sources. We must live our lives from the inside out, not from the outside in as we have been doing. The only true source of good feelings is within us.

Learning to Value Ourselves

Before we can have loving relationships with others, we must develop loving relationships with ourselves. Many of us have neglected and abused ourselves because of our addictions. We came to hate ourselves and discounted our value as we became more isolated and out of touch with our lives. We were no longer fully alive; we were dying inside. We need to learn to value ourselves for who we are. Initially, we may not know who we are, but as we nurture our budding new selves, we discover qualities within that we have either forgotten or overlooked. Many of us easily identify qualities we despise about ourselves. Yet, within them, at least there is always a seed of strength.

For example, we may know of our perfectionism and recognize the negative consequences. However, we may not see the positive aspects of perfectionism: caring, diligence, and a desire to achieve and do better. Perfectionism is an example of losing perspective on what is truly important as a result of our underlying insecurity. Sometimes, we judge our positive qualities as insignificant. Consider the person who has a delightful sense of humor, yet is unable to see how this can contribute to a healthy lifestyle or a loving relationship.

As we develop personal recovery programs through the Twelve Steps, we begin to see the need to take care of ourselves, and we learn about our capabilities and potentials. This is less a matter of building self-esteem than it is a matter of clearing up, calming down, and liberating the natural good feelings that were locked inside us before. The process of addiction was our innocent search for wholeness. In the beginning, our efforts appeared to be successful to some degree, or we would not have continued. However, our addictions or compulsions were external solutions; we were living life from the outside in. Through recovery, we are learning who we are, and we are able to love ourselves in spite of our imperfections. It is more helpful to accentuate and nurture our positive qualities rather than dwell on our negative ones.

Awareness of a Higher Power

An integral part of coming to love ourselves arises from a developing awareness of a Power greater than ourselves. This awareness is the cornerstone of true self-esteem. It provides an unshakable foundation on which to build loving relationships with ourselves and others. It does not matter what we name this Power; some call it God, others Divine Consciousness, and others have called it the Force. There are countless other names. It is clear this Power is not only external but also exists within, however aware or unaware of it we may be.

The result of our growing awareness of a Higher Power, as well as our consciousness of our own natural self-esteem, is that we become capable of forming truly loving relationships with others. As we become more involved with others in healthy ways, we gain further insights into ourselves and our Higher Power. These three areas—our Higher Power, others, and ourselves—are so interwoven that progress in one area can also be seen in the other two areas.

The foundation of a loving relationship is a quiet mind, bringing a sense of serenity. Our minds are quiet when they are free of the continual mental chatter we often indulge in, without realizing such thoughts are the source of our pain and unhappiness. Much of this chatter—our mental radio—is derived from those old belief systems we're so attached to. When we begin to quiet this inner dialogue, we allow our natural wisdom to come forth, and we become more receptive to insights. With a quiet, clear mind we can begin to dream new dreams. We can envision loving relationships for ourselves.

One thing that will help us drop these old beliefs and quiet our minds is the ability to laugh, both at ourselves and with others. A sense of humor will allow us to take ourselves less seriously and to gain a more realistic perspective on our problems and capabilities.

Many of us have been engulfed in resentments we've directed toward ourselves or others. When we learn to take ourselves and the world less seriously and see that many of our judgments have been based on the old and faulty beliefs, our ability to forgive is enhanced.

Gratitude is essential. Focusing on what is right in our lives and in the world creates a feeling of gratitude. When we are grateful, we tend to believe in ourselves more. We're more self-confident and find it easier to take risks, allowing ourselves to be vulnerable. It is only from this position that we can enter into a truly loving relationship.

Focusing on Positive Thoughts

Within our loving relationships, we must continue our efforts to grow in all areas of our lives. It is important to see the role of thought in our well-being. We all have thoughts, and our thoughts create the realities in which we live. However, we often forget we are the thinker. We fail to realize our feelings are the result of our attitudes or beliefs. A danger lies in seeing our thoughts as facts, taking them as inescapable reality. We can become entangled in these thoughts. How we perceive things depends on the emotional state we are in. For example, if we are in a negative mood, we will likely hear an innocent remark as a personal putdown. It is helpful for us to be aware of our negative moods and how they affect the way we see the world around us.

Our minds are clearer when we feel good, and we are less likely to be confused by the details of our problems. We can take a larger view of the situation and act from a higher level of awareness. We begin to see that we don't have to make ourselves feel good; we only have to stop making ourselves feel bad. Good feelings are inherent.

On the spiritual level, we must nurture our inner wisdom—that still, small voice that many of us have spent years ignoring. We must learn to listen to this voice; it is our connection to our Higher Power. The quieter our minds are, the more we hear this voice and open up to insights that allow us to create lasting love and health for ourselves.

Part of loving ourselves is treating our bodies with respect. When we are listening to our inner wisdom, this respect is merely a matter of common sense. We know we must get enough rest, eat properly, and exercise regularly. If we find ourselves in a bad mood, we may be overtired and may simply need a nap. Perhaps we have been so busy our eating habits have been irregular, and we need to have a nutritious meal. And it has been said that exercise is the best remedy for depression. Clearly, when we are not feeling good physically, it affects the way we think, the way we feel emotionally, and the way we interact with others.

As our relationships with ourselves develop and we become healthier, we renew old friendships and form new ones. Friendships are loving relationships and are an essential part of life. They help prepare us for a more meaningful loving relationship. In fact, friendship is the vital ingredient of the significant, deeper loving relationship we are seeking.

Respecting Another's Differences

When we are falling in love we see the other person as perfect, or we ignore his or her faults. We are filled with exhilaration. We see the world through rose-colored glasses. We attribute our good feelings to the presence of that other person in our life. But, most of us have not realized these feelings come from within ourselves. The other person is only a catalyst.

As the relationship continues, the intense feelings may fade. We may experience renewed fears of intimacy and become more insecure. We then become judgmental and begin to focus on each other's imperfections. The more seriously we take these judgments, the more we will blame the other for our negative feelings. Our old beliefs and attitudes can easily resurface. For example, we may find ourselves thinking, ''I'm not capable of a good relationship, I don't deserve one.'' Or we may make sweeping generalizations, such as ''men can't be trusted,'' ''women can't be trusted,'' ''relationships never last.'' When we catch ourselves being judgmental of others, we need to remember we each have our own way of looking at things. These are only thoughts, and we have a choice of how seriously we want to take them.

We all see the world from a special point of view, and we each may draw entirely different conclusions about the same event. We often expect others to see things our way, and we waste hours in frustration trying to convince them of our views. We may have forgotten that some of those differences were the elements that helped us fall in love. If this happens to us, we are losing our perspective and beginning to take our thoughts too seriously.

Letting go of our attempts to control another is a remedy for this. We can let go of trying to make this person into something he or she is not. We can begin to appreciate our personality differences once again and see the richness the other can bring to our life by sharing unique perceptions. We need to cultivate gratitude within the relationship by focusing on what we like about it. We can even find value in aspects of the relationship that we are least comfortable with. When we look at what we can learn from this, we are more apt to feel grateful and forgiving. We can accept this person. The more accepting and forgiving we are of ourselves, the more accepting and forgiving we will be of another.

Living in the Present

Our relationship with our Higher Power is strengthened through involvement with others in Twelve Step programs. We hear wisdom we can use by listening to others as they deal with their problems. One of the most valuable principles we are reminded of in Twelve Step programs is living one day at a time. This helps us live fully in the moment, which is an essential part of living in an intimate relationship. All we really have is the moment. If we are crippled by past memories or frightened by future worries, we miss the beauty of relationships and of the day as it unfolds. We also become more disconnected from who we are. Living in the moment takes faith in ourselves, others, and our Higher Power.

We are always changing. Living in the present allows us to see each other more clearly, unhampered by our past judgments or future expectations of others. We can be closer to others when we live in the moment. We see one another in a new light, and we are able to celebrate our differences and similarities when we live one day at a time.

Loving relationships are possible for us, and all relationships can be loving. A healthy relationship is distinguished by the awareness that we *choose* to be there rather than believing we *need* to be there. We must love ourselves, have faith in a Higher Power, and respect others. None of us will do this perfectly all of the time. But we can learn to be gentle with ourselves and know we strive for progress not perfection. And every day we learn.

FORGIVENESS

Early in recovery we experienced the healing and freedom of forgiveness.

We often heard about forgiveness when we were practicing our addiction—we thought it was great for those who needed it. However, one of our goals in life was to avoid needing it. We felt like the man who said, "I'd admit my faults if I had any!"

The principles of the Twelve Steps began changing all that. Steps Four and Ten, especially, helped us take a look at ourselves and encouraged us to take our own inventories. What clicked for us was the truth of the question, "Why, then, do you look at the speck in your brother's eye and pay no attention to the log in your own eye?" (Good News Bible, Today's English Version, Matthew 7:3). We discovered we had very good skills at taking inventories—but they were usually directed at someone else. We began to understand the saying in the Program: "Take *your own* inventory."

So we took our own inventories. And then the forgiveness we used to admire in others began to knock at our spiritual doorstep. We discovered many new things about forgiveness for ourselves.

Self-Forgiveness

Gradually, a painful truth became clear to us: We found that to be human is to need forgiveness. For many of us this was very painful. The "oughts" and the "shoulds" tripped us up: "We ought not need forgiveness," "We should not have behaved that way—even if we were out of control!" We even laid guilt trips on ourselves for having guilt! Many of us rebelled by saying, "But I don't deserve forgiveness."

Through the fellowship of love and caring dawned the principle that forgiveness is never earned or deserved—it is *freely given*. Forgiveness is *for giving*. And, paradoxically, we have to do something wrong in order to have this worthwhile experience.

But the task of forgiving ourselves remained monumental. Our self-esteem was at its lowest; our spiritual resources were still new. We kept going to meetings, and began to see ourselves in others. We learned we had not committed any unusual wrongs. We also learned two basic attitudes embodied in the principle of forgiveness.

We heard others describe their pasts—just as marred and irresponsible as our own—with a sense of peace and serenity. They were no longer stooped over with the burden of guilt; they held their heads up. When we asked how this could be, we were told it could come about by letting go of the grudge we held against ourselves. Those who were religious sought this forgiveness, or letting go, through a church, synagogue, etc.

When we did not find instant relief, many of us felt

it was too difficult and we'd never be able to do it. "There's got to be something wrong with me," or, "It worked for them, but not for me," were common statements. Then we were reminded of the nature of spirituality; it is a *process* more than an event, at least it seems so for most of us. We learned to be "willing to grow along (forgiveness) lines." We would grow into being forgiven.

We also discovered that, perhaps, the most difficult part was *accepting* forgiveness from others. Accepting forgiveness involves forgiving self: it *is* forgiving self. At first it was easy for many of us to believe and mouth all the right words. However, it wasn't so easy to pocket our pride and go to it; namely, to accept forgiveness for ourselves on a personal level. Many of us asked our Higher Power for help. For awhile, some even asked on a daily basis.

As we worked on our inventory, admitting our shortcomings to God, ourselves, and another human being, and sought spiritual help to be rid of these defects, we discovered the burden of guilt did lighten. We found relief; some found it more quickly than others. But, it came. We began to see ourselves as human and in need of forgiveness, and the war within became stilled. We let go. The past was at rest.

Self-Acceptance

Accepting ourselves *as we are*, as imperfect human beings, has been of central importance in our recovery. This fact will not change! Again, for some of us, this proves to be a real challenge until we let go absolutely. Although we are free of our bad feelings about our past behavior, grandiosity often overcomes us with the attitude that we're different. In short, we're saying, I needed forgiveness for my past but I'll never need it again because I'm going to change into someone who doesn't need it.

This, of course, is our perfectionism talking; *what we are* never equals what we think we *should* or *ought to be*. Our tendency is to make self-acceptance conditional. We reason, I'll accept myself only if I am as I think I should or ought to be. And so we're doomed to self-condemnation. Our perfectionism keeps us thinking, I am never good enough. Therefore, I am not acceptable.

Again, the Fellowship helps us out. Steps Six and Seven ask that we be willing to change and grow, and that the decision about that, and the power for it, lay in the hands of our Higher Power. When we asked Him "to remove our shortcomings," He may have decided to leave us with a few. What matters is that we are willing to have them removed. The message remains: We are unconditionally accepted by the God of our understanding, shortcomings and all!

Who do we think we are to judge ourselves as unacceptable? Here dawns another spiritual awareness: We are our own worst judges! If we are going to accept ourselves, we need to accept ourselves totally and unconditionally. We need to befriend those aspects we have so hated and condemned. We can accept that we are in the hands of a Power much greater than ourselves; a Higher Power who knows and accepts us *as we are*. From this we draw the faith and the boldness to do it for ourselves, too. We find that we are able to describe our past with our heads held high and a sense of peace inside.

Forgiving Others

Early in recovery we developed an attitude of forgiveness in our relationships at meetings. We listened nonjudgmentally as newcomers told their stories. Most of us did not find this too difficult since we did not have a personal investment.

Forgiving others whose actions affect us personally (in reality or in our imaginations) is more difficult. Here our resentments show; in some cases we harbor grudges a long time. In fact, we've even discovered that occasionally the grudge is so long-standing we forgot what the initial offense was. As a result, we substitute the person for the offense. This attitude was well-stated by one grudge-bearing soul: "I don't know why, but I don't like him." Grudges tend to magnify and generalize with time. We find forgiveness most effective when we are specific with the subject.

Some of us balk at forgiving others saying they don't deserve it. Until we recognize this as a relentless resentment we stay unwilling to forgive, and also quite unhappy. Others resist forgiving another because we believe it won't do any good anyway—she'll never change.

What clears the air is the realization that forgiving changes the heart of the *forgiver*, but may not change the forgiven at all. This is another spiritual awakening: We can help our own healing by forgiving another. We recall clearly how our resentments kept us awake at night, or kept us unhappy, negative, and angry while the one we resented slept peacefully and lived more serenely than we. We are aware that we are prisoners of our own resentments, and that our forgiving another really unlocks the door and sets us free.

At this point some of us are brought to our knees

again to ask for help. We want that freedom, but the necessary change in attitude is so elusive and difficult to achieve. Some of us are drawn back to the old attitude, thinking, But it's not fair that I should have to do the forgiving. They should be asking *me* to forgive *them*! We need to keep asking ourselves, Am I *willing to go to any length* to get personal peace and freedom from resentment?

Getting Our Lists in Order

Step Eight suggests we list all the people we've harmed. Very often the first draft of our list contains the names of people we truly believe have harmed us. And, perhaps they have. However, the problem is that this very belief blinds us to our part in it.

There is a suggestion in our fellowship that has helped at least a few of us: If it's as much as one-half our fault, then we need to include our part on the list and omit the fault of the other. Doing Step Eight and sharing with sponsors and others has helped many of us sort out our own hurt and anger. Our own shame and guilt over harming someone else in turn harmed us.

In an attempt to discover our one-half fault, our spiritual self-perception grows miraculously. We can see our fault more clearly. Many of us find, much to our surprise, that we have contributed much more to the problem than we first thought. In sorting out our roles, Step Nine helps us make amends where appropriate.

We continue to grow spiritually as we seek help to forgive "through prayer and meditation." For some of us the growth is helped by the Serenity Prayer, especially when we reword it, "God, grant me the serenity to (forgive) the (behavior of others), courage to change the (behavior I can, namely, my own), and the wisdom to know the difference.''

We also receive help in the petition from the Lord's Prayer to ''Forgive us our trespasses *as* we forgive those who trespass against us.''

Some of us gain freedom by praying for those we resent. We ask that good things be given to them. We experience a ''letting go'' when we find we cannot resent someone while praying for him or her. We might ask that the person be blessed with the warmth of our love and acceptance. Furthermore, we can pray until it becomes a reality. Then we know we have forgiven, and we are free of those ill feelings.

Forgiving and accepting ourselves and others opens us up to love and closeness with them. This is what we were looking for all the time!

As time goes on, however, we discover we are ''permanently'' human. Many of us are dismayed when our negative behaviors begin to show up again—even in a few days! There must be something wrong with us, we think, as the old self-condemning thinking once again raises its ugly head.

Checking Up

From the Fellowship comes the suggestion to do Step Ten. This Step, we are told, can help us keep our ''forgiving'' tuned up. It suggests that we continue to take personal inventory and admit our wrongs. Those who have worked the Program before us say they do this because they have not reached perfection. This is comforting and strengthening; they, too, are permanently human. They need to inventory attitudes, behaviors, and relationships on a regular basis; and be willing to ask for forgiveness and be forgiving. This helps them stay healthy.

If it works for them, won't it work for us? We realize that ignoring our mistakes and faults and blaming others does not work for us; it has kept us codependent, or trapped in the addictive process.

Some of us inventory our behavior every day before leaving for work, school, or prior to our main activities. We ask ourselves, How are my attitudes toward my loved ones? We can examine our attitudes and conduct toward our friends, coworkers, and peers from the Fellowship. This provides an outline for doing Step Ten daily.

Our experiences with forgiveness remove many barriers between ourselves and others. Our unreasonable fears of being found out or hurt by others leave us; we can receive and give love, and learn to trust others.

Renewing Contact

As our loving relationships grow more nurturing and supportive, we look toward Step Eleven to bring us a closer relationship with the God of our understanding.

In the past many of us were so burdened by guilt and feelings of worthlessness that a close personal relationship with a God of our understanding seemed incomprehensible. Some had a forbidding concept of God—a tyrannical God who would surely do us in at the time of reckoning. Some of us had heard of a loving God, but we couldn't trust such a God. Many of us reasoned that God wasn't loving after all, or, if He were, then we didn't deserve His love.

Forgiveness changed that. By removing our self-condemnation we experience unconditional love and acceptance. A great number of us have come to believe in the "loving God" of Tradition Two. We learned that with "prayer and meditation" we can gain a closer, conscious relationship with the God of our understanding.

Forgiveness awards us clear lines of communication with our Higher Power. We can consult for "His will for us and the power to carry that out." Many of us find that His will for us is recovery. Thus, whatever changes in our lives, behaviors, and relationships have helped us maintain abstinence are clearly "His will for us." This includes maintaining forgiveness as our way of life. Where we once found asking for forgiveness impossible, and the grace to forgive others elusive, the presence of God's will has brought us the humility to ask and the grace to give.

Yes—we have not arrived—but *we have made progress*. For that we are grateful, a gift freely given to us. We do have a spiritual awakening by doing these Steps. And having done the self-care work of forgiveness—receiving and giving—and claiming a program of spiritual Steps to maintain us, we are ready for Step Twelve. We are asked once again to look beyond *self*-care to the care *for selves* (others).

As many of us look back at our beginnings in the Fellowship, we realize we would have been turned off by condescending, unforgiving attitudes. Fortunately, we were met with love and acceptance; those who greeted us truly carried the message. They assured us that they, too, had been there. A daily reprieve, they said, was all they had. We knew we were with folks just like us. There was just something in the way they accepted us.

One quality of forgiveness many of us discover is that

it unites us with all of humanity. We are united in our need to be forgiven and in our need to be forgiving. The very unity of our Fellowship depends upon this.

ACCEPTING
CRITICISM

THE INABILITY TO ACCEPT CRITICISM RANKS HIGH ON our list of character defects and appears on most Fourth Step inventories. Many of us explode with anger and resentment at the slightest suggestion we may be wrong. "Stop criticizing me!" we snap. "You're not perfect either, you know!" Even though no one asked us to be perfect, or claimed to be perfect themselves, our hurt feelings make us strike back. Before we know it, we have a mini-war on our hands, and there will be no winner.

How can we deal with this explosive feeling and avoid creating unhappiness for ourselves and others? Probably the best way is to see criticism as a tool for growth rather than a weapon of attack. Bill W., co-founder of Alcoholics Anonymous (A.A.), once observed that A.A. would have progressed more slowly without its strong critics. He also expressed appreciation for his own critics, saying some taught him patience, while others offered him "valuable lessons." Bill's sane and sensible reaction to criticism is a model for all of us.

Criticism is an Inside Job

The first thing to remember about criticism is that we do it to ourselves. If we are stabbed by a critical remark, we are doing the stabbing. This may seem surprising, but it's true. For example, if we're told we have poor taste in clothes, we can choose to believe it and think we really are poor dressers, or we can reject the remark as untrue, irrelevant, unimportant, or uninformed.

If we don't agree, we won't be hurt; what others say just won't be true (as we see it). We may wonder what's the matter with them, and look for what's going on inside their heads to provoke a comment like that. We may even feel sorry they should be so mistaken. We can react in a variety of ways to this kind of statement.

Only when we accept the criticism as valid can we become vulnerable to hurt. Then we take the words to heart and feel the sting inside. The hurt comes when our inner voice says, I'm so ashamed, or, How embarrassing to be so stupid! In this case, *we're* criticizing *ourselves*.

When we're criticized, we often learn more about the critic than ourselves. Remember the story of the psychiatrist and the teenage boy? The doctor drew a circle on a sheet of paper and asked the boy, "What does that remind you of?" "Sex," he replied. The doctor next drew a square, and asked the same question. "Sex," repeated the young man. The doctor then drew a triangle, and once more got the answer, "Sex." You seem to have sex on your mind," the doctor observed. "I do?" the boy replied. "You're the one who keeps drawing the dirty pictures!"

The point is, before we get upset and angry, we need to consider the source. Imagine a telephone lineman telling a registered nurse what kind of anesthesia a surgeon should use for an operation, or the nurse telling the lineman how to install a telephone switchboard! It would certainly be foolish for either one to take such suggestions seriously or be disturbed by them for even a moment.

However, we can't always reply, "You're entitled to your opinion and I'm entitled to mine," for criticism may be deserved, and also helpful, as Bill W. pointed out. Once we get ego out of the way—and that's what we've been talking about—criticism need not be such a bad or painful thing. It can, in fact, be quite useful. How? For one thing, it can give us a fresh look at ourselves.

Mirror Image

Even the most introspective person can be blind to some of the truths about him- or herself. Years of self-analysis fail to expose the obvious if we have a prejudice or a blind spot. A person who doesn't know proper grammar might naturally say, "Them that doesn't wants to doesn't has to." He wouldn't criticize this sentence; to his ear it sounds correct. At a moment like this it helps to have a friend correct him in a tactful way. This is particularly true if he is hoping to make a good impression on those who *do* use good grammar!

Helpful criticism lets us see where our biases, lack of information, or lack of self-awareness keep us blind. We will never know all there is to know about ourselves; human beings never do. Criticism helps complete us.

This is the motivation behind the Fourth and Fifth Steps. We have learned that lack of self-knowledge is a chief stumbling block to recovery, abstinence, or sanity. Bill wrote that the ones who fail are those who are "constitutionally incapable of being honest with themselves." The experience of countless Twelve Step group members teaches the same thing. "The Program won't work until you start getting honest with yourself." "I had to get honest before I could ever get into recovery." "Honesty is the key." We hear these words and others like them over and over again.

Such advice is not uttered to frighten or discourage anyone; it is a practical insight and an accurate description of just what it takes to "make it" in the Program. Doing the Fourth Step inventory and admitting all we have found out about ourselves to another human being is one sure way of getting honest. The one who hears our Fifth Step acts as a mirror, showing us what we really look like, not just how we would like to appear. When we get a more accurate picture of who and what we are, we can use our talents and skills more effectively and avoid some of our more glaring defects.

When we first started recovery, many of us didn't really understand why we acted the way we did. We felt our minds and bodies were booby-trapped with spiritual and emotional "land mines" that could go off at any time. We didn't know what or where they were. It was quite impossible to live each day wondering when we would trigger one of them again. The Program blessed us with the wisdom of the inventory and of talking it over with someone else. We may not get rid of all the "mines," but we can learn where they are and how to avoid or defuse them.

Another human being can guide us to some of the "mines." His or her objective eye can help us see ourselves, and we, in turn, can be just as helpful to others. We are mirrors for each other!

Double-Edged Sword

When we submit to criticism, or offer it to others, we must remember we are dealing with a dangerous tool. "You know where you stand with me!" one young woman proudly announced because she was "only being honest" with others. It sounded commendable, but she really used this as an excuse to say whatever she felt without thinking about other people's feelings. Her remarks were not helpful; they hurt, and they came from a reservoir of hurt inside her which she either didn't recognize or refused to admit was there. This was not honest reflection, it was hostile attack. Such remarks should be seen for what they are. If we take such words to heart they will cut and destroy.

One way to avoid hurting others is to speak from our feelings rather than judging their behavior. There's a world of difference between saying, "I get uncomfortable when you swear so often," and "You ought to stop cussing; it isn't nice." The first statement can be a scalpel that exposes a character defect; the second is a meat-ax that will probably make the problem worse. When we speak about our feelings without trying to make someone else feel ashamed or guilty we are offering useful criticism. In other words, "Don't take other people's inventory."

Criticism is a tool for determining value. It is a standard for judging and can be used to improve performance. Athletes in training are subjected to criticism in order to discover their weak points and perform better. Authors submit their work to critics to see how well they have accomplished their task. Golfers listen to the advice of friends in hopes of bettering their golf score. This is the purpose of criticism.

The problem comes when we interpret criticism as a

diminishment of our value. If our efforts are criticized, we are no good. Someone points out that I made a grammatical error and I respond, "I *never* do anything right!" The criticism, which was only a tool to evaluate a particular effort, is taken as a judgment from the gods. It sounds as if I were saying, "If you don't love my sentence, you don't love me and therefore I'm no good!" That's a lot to assume from one criticism.

When we state how we feel rather than point out others' possible shortcomings, we can avoid hurting them. We also help ourselves if we avoid making a remark sound like a total condemnation. Being aware of the significance of what we say keeps the sword of criticism in balance.

The Measuring Stick

Every criticism implies a value judgment. A simple remark like, "You're late!" only makes sense if we both know what "on time" means. If one person thinks 10:30 P.M. is the right time to be home, while another assumes 1:00 A.M. is the deadline, there can be no agreement. The problem is agreeing on the definition of "on time."

Much criticism can be troublesome because we aren't using the same measuring stick. For example, a frustrated mother explodes when she sees her son's bedroom. "It's a disaster!" she cries. Knowing she wants everything neat and tidy all the time, the angry adolescent protests the unfair criticism. "You expect me to be perfect!" They're both talking about the same room, but each sees it differently. A common measuring stick would help.

Some think criticism has quite a bit to do with perfection. Anything less than perfect is imperfect, and that, by definition, is bad. If criticism is applied as a tool to achieve perfection, the one being criticized cannot help but feel judged, devalued, belittled.

Actually criticism has little to do with perfection; it's an impossible goal, so it's useless to expect perfection from someone. Measuring anything against perfection proves nothing. Critical remarks are much more helpful if we make them with a more realistic measuring stick.

Telling stories from experience can be a positive and productive way of criticizing. "Well, when I was in a spot like that, here's what happened to me." Bill W. used this method very effectively. This supports the tradition of "attraction rather than promotion." If we show others the benefits of our experience, they can make a choice that might work for them. This way they won't feel coerced, devalued, or judged.

The Measure of Love

Probably the biggest problem with criticism—whether we are receiving it or giving it—is the problem of personal ego. We know what's best for ourselves and others based on personal criteria and preferences. When we decide someone needs to change his hairstyle, we may very well believe it's in his best interest; but this really is a question of personal opinion. He might interpret our words as criticism and condemnation instead of a helpful hint. He might respond with his opinion, which he feels is every bit as good as ours. From this point on there is no hope for growth. We end up arguing over who's the smartest, has the best taste, or the most convincing experience. The result will be anger, hurt feelings, and probably a broken relationship.

How do we avoid this impasse? In my experience, the most helpful rule is the measure of love. When I speak, I do so in love. I speak as a friend. I speak as one conscious of your best qualities. For that is what it means to love—to see infinite value and worth in others.

Love is not a sentimental emotion for greeting cards; it is a special vision that sees beauty where others do not see it and recognizes worth others have overlooked. We might notice a couple that seems very strangely matched and asked, "What on earth does she see in him (or he in her)?" The fact is they *do* see worth in each other, and that is the meaning of love. There is value and goodness there which we admire, enjoy, and want to encourage.

All of us have been on the receiving end of love if we have found our way to the Program. Whether our problem was alcohol or other drugs, overeating, gambling, or codependency, we agonized in the knowledge that we were flawed, no good. We were told we had great potential, but we could not fulfill that potential. We felt worse for knowing how far short we fell of our own ideals.

Then we encountered people with the same problems—and they were making it. With the help of our Higher Power we began to bloom and grow; and with the encouragement of these friends our problems lessened and hope no longer seemed out of reach. What was happening to us was the healing of love. People saw good in us we could not see; they placed faith in us we did not have in ourselves.

Criticism is only valid if born of the keen eyesight of love. Those who criticize us in order to help us be more true to ourselves, speak in love. Those who criticize so they can show us how much better or smarter they are, or how much better they are at living their lives than we are, are not real critics. They are trying to make themselves feel better at our expense, and we don't have to listen or accept their words.

By the same token, criticism from us should contain the same vision of goodness in others. If we see no worth in someone, we have no right to criticize. We are truly blind and our opinion has no value.

God's Children

We are all God's children and each of us is a person of infinite worth. When we deal with others, our task is to look for the treasure buried within. And the more we see in others, the more others will uncover treasures in us. Criticism will no longer be a brutal blow to our ego; it will be an adventure of treasure hunting.

Criticism may still be painful, of course. Growth always is. It is humiliating to have our defects and shortcomings pointed out to us—we all prefer compliments to blame. On the other hand, being confronted with a bit of truth about ourselves is the biggest help we can get. When we are criticized, the wise thing to do is search for whatever truth it contains. A quick "spot inventory" as Bill recommends in Step Ten, can validate the criticism and show us whether this is a place for growth, or an opportunity to show our true selves to others. A visit with our sponsor, or a discussion with friends at a meeting, can help us see more clearly where wisdom lies.

Genuine criticism tells us we are all God's children and have value and worth; it is the clear-eyed look of love. It can give us a glimpse of what we are and what we can be. With that vision we are healed and enabled to grow. If we can remember this we need never fear criticism. In fact, we can be grateful for its gift!

LETTING GO

A WEALTH OF WISDOM AND EXPERIENCE LIES BEHIND the simple A.A. saying—"let go." The following story illustrates how we hinder our spiritual progress when we refuse to let go.

One day two monks were walking through the woods on their way to help gather the autumn harvest in the next village. As they approached a small stream, they met an old woman from their village sitting upon the bank. The first monk asked her, "Grete, what are you doing, sitting here wringing your hands? I thought you were supposed to be at your son's house just after dawn today to help with the apple pressing."

Grete answered, "I am afraid to cross the stream, even though I know it is but a trifle, a small splash of water. I suppose I am a foolish old woman. So I have been sitting here these last hours, wringing my hands and wondering what to do."

The first monk said to her, "We will carry you across this small stream." The two monks joined their hands to fashion a seat and carried her safely across the water. Then the monks continued on their way.

One mile later, the second monk said to the first, "My frock is wet and soiled because of that foolish old woman. And my back still hurts from the strain of carrying her." The first monk just smiled and said nothing.

Three miles later, the second monk said, "My back is still sore and aching. I know I shall have trouble helping with the harvest today." Again, the first monk smiled and said nothing.

Five miles later, the second monk complained, "I am sure now that you will have to go ahead without me. My back aches so much because of that foolish old woman, that I cannot travel any farther."

The first monk turned to the second monk and said, "Your back aches because you are still carrying her. I let go five miles ago when I put her down on the other side of the stream."

Fighting the Program

At some point in our recovery, all of us experience the struggle of letting go. Like the second monk, we cling to old habits or resentments that make our progress forward difficult or even impossible. When we encounter impasses in our recovery, we summon our old stubbornness and pride and hopelessly thrash about, like fish scooped up by fishermen's nets. We continue struggling, thinking we must fight alone. We call this "fighting the program."

Fighting the program means living from a "me" instead of "we" perspective. While we were practicing addicts, we felt we carried the problems of the whole world on our shoulders, and we could never put away our worries, even for a moment. Instead, we laid awake at night scheming about how to manipulate situations, or worrying about potential catastrophes.

Old habits die slowly. After we achieve some abstinence, we are often surprised that many of our troubles remain. We can no longer escape to the magic freedom of the bottle, pills, food, or sex where all our problems seem to disappear. We experience many old feelings of shame and remorse over past binges, as well as regrets about failed relationships. These feelings haunt us with an intensity we hadn't known while we were numbed by addiction.

When we are confronted with unpleasant feelings and the necessity to change, we may fall back on our deepest instinct—we fight. We clench our teeth and determine through sheer willpower to get ourselves out of this mess. But like a car spinning its tires in the snow, our struggle only makes the situation worse.

Whether the problem is to quit smoking, or quit sugar, or move on after a relationship ends, we cannot change as long as we struggle. Fighting the program means clinging to old ways in spite of ourselves, even when we want to change.

Why do we do this? Change is frightening. The past may have been miserable, but at least it was familiar. We become comfortable with old habits and thought patterns which keep us from growing. Letting go of them can be as painful and difficult as giving up our addictions or compulsions.

Our negative thoughts can snowball and, at times, consume us. Negative thinking separates us from a sense of belonging, suffocates our hope and prevents us from gaining true happiness. Negativity has been a part of our lives for so many years, we need a great deal of practice to develop positive views.

If we pause in the midst of our struggles and worries,

we can give ourselves time to let a new realization sink in: we don't *have* to fight anymore. We have another choice: we can surrender. Rather than manipulating situations, we can surrender control. Surrender is essentially an act of trust. When we let go, we can trust events to unfold on their own. Trust gives us a sense of acceptance, and through acceptance we find serenity.

Paradoxically, surrender is not the same as giving up. When we first came to the program, we didn't give up. We surrendered to our illness. Instead of trying to control, we asked for help. Surrender means exchanging "me" for "we." Surrender means letting go.

If I Let Go, Who Will Catch Me?

Many of us cling to old habits and problems, even though we realize they cause more harm than good. Deep in our hearts we feel alone in the world. In the program we find a glimmer of hope that we are *not* alone. We find a fellowship of men and women to share our strengths, experiences, and hopes. We listen to the suggestions of older members instead of dismissing ideas that differed from ours.

Gaining a sense of connection with others helps build a spiritual foundation that will sustain us in times of trouble. Before finding the program, we felt we were perched on the edge of a great cliff, ready to fall at any moment. We clung desperately to the little we had left of our lives to avoid tumbling into the blackness of insanity or death. We were afraid to live and afraid to die.

How could we let go if we had nowhere to go and no one to catch us? We led trapped and desperate lives. In recovery we need to occasionally remind ourselves how far we have come and how much we have to be grateful for. It's easy to slip into old ways of thinking during times of stress and look for impulsive, desperate, or easy solutions. We need to remember we now have more options than we had previously thought imaginable. We no longer have to play the trapped victim or the master puppeteer who tries to control the lives of all those around him. We can be human, with all the freedom which that brings.

When we are confronted with a problem and feel afraid, we can remember we are part of the fellowship; we can find strength in realizing we no longer need to battle our personal dragons alone. We can pause, allow the panic to subside, and listen to our inner voices. This time of quietness helps us break the walls of our loneliness and find a sense of connection with our Higher Power. We remember to "Let go and let God."

Our Higher Power will help us in times of need. By cultivating a positive attitude of faith and hope we can put our problems in perspective. Times of pain are always opportunities for growth, and our Higher Power never gives us more than we can handle. We don't need to solve all our problems in a day; we don't have to solve all our problems by ourselves. All we need to do is reach beyond ourselves, through meditation and prayer, and talk things over with a sponsor or friend. We can let go, secure in the fact that our Higher Power and the fellowship will help and support us.

Getting Ready

Most of us are not able to immediately surrender control of our problems to our Higher Power. We often struggle until we become so miserable that we throw up our hands and cry, "I give up!"

We don't need to struggle until we reach the depths of misery. Warning signs can make us aware of when we need to "Let go and let God." When we become increasingly irritable with friends, coworkers, or our family, we may be taking everyone's inventory but our own. We may imagine solutions such as, "If only this person would change, then I could finally be happy."

Patterns of being overly critical and controlling usually mean we are avoiding taking a good hard look at ourselves. We may be ignoring a character defect. It's easier to blame our problems on someone else. When we let go of our efforts to change other people, we take responsibility for our own growth and change. We can turn things around by realizing we are not the center of the universe. Like snowflakes, we are each separate and unique. Instead of wasting energy criticizing others, we can let go and appreciate their specialness.

Isolation is another warning that tells us to let go. We begin to miss meetings, or we switch meetings so we are no longer responsible to a home group. We may begin to call friends less, and we make up excuses when invited out. We may isolate ourselves by talking to only one special friend.

We often isolate ourselves when we feel secretly ashamed about a problem. We may be in an abusive or overly dependent relationship. We may have an eating disorder, become compulsive shoppers, or gamblers. Whatever the problem, the first step is to reach out to our Higher Power and other people.

We begin by being honest with ourselves and others. At meetings, we talk honestly about our struggles in working the Twelve Steps. We are honest with friends instead of telling them everything is fine. We need to be gentle with ourselves and patient with our Higher Power. The pain of personal growth is part of the human experience. While going through painful periods, we can be good to ourselves. Take a bubble bath, go for a walk with a friend, go to a movie, or curl up with a good book.

When we let go, we need to remember our Higher Power doesn't work miracles if we sit back and do nothing. We need to pray for potatoes with hoes in our hands. For example, a salesman who had a few months of recovery had to give a sales presentation. He was terrified at the prospect of speaking in front of a large group of his peers, so he decided to "let go and let God." He prayed to his Higher Power for courage, then spent the night watching television instead of preparing for the presentation.

His presentation did not go well. At his Twelve Step meeting, the salesman complained that "This letting go stuff isn't all that it's cracked up to be." But, by the end of the meeting the salesman realized that instead of letting go of his anxieties, he had let go of his responsibilities. Letting go is not a license to be lazy or irresponsible. Letting go is an admission of humility and faith, followed by action!

Letting go helps us live with our problems and with our disease. We admitted we were powerless and our lives had become unmanageable; we turned our will over to the care of God as we understood Him. This means we live one day at a time; we go to meetings, and we try to work the Twelve Steps to the best of our ability. We pray for potatoes with hoes in our hands.

Accepting Change

When we let go we accept the fact that life is constantly changing. Yesterday's joys and sorrows are past. If we cling to the past, we miss the wonder and excitement of the present. We go through our lives in a trance.

When we are confronted with a problem which seems insurmountable, we may look back to the past through rose-colored glasses. Life seemed sweeter, simpler, and easier. We may feel the pain of an old relationship and brood about how wonderful life was. We feel trapped by our memories, and find we can't stop thinking about them.

We need to take a leap of faith. Letting go means having faith that we are put in this world to experience life fully. We can lead useful, productive, and happy lives. When we put our lives into the care of our Higher Power, we can truly look at the world around us. We may realize how unaware of our surroundings we have been while mired in depression and hopelessness. A miracle happens when we are willing to change and to live in the present. We discover people are there ready and waiting to help us.

Letting go of negative attitudes is manageable if we concentrate on living one day at a time. Living one day at a time puts our problems into perspective and reminds us that a well-lived life begins in the present, not in the past or future.

The ability to accept change is the gift we receive when we let go. Simple acts of faith and humility give us much in return. We exchange our sad, gray ''me's'' for exciting, multicolored ''we's.'' We discover tolerance for people who look or act differently than we do. We form friendships and are intimate without the constant, fruitless struggle of trying to change others.

We can laugh, cry, and celebrate the miracle of life together. We have let go, and by letting go have gained a precious gift. We accept our own and other's frailties, and we grow from our pain. This ability to learn from our experiences is part of the miracle of the program. We turned our weakness into our greatest strength; by letting go we gained an understanding of the spiritual principles of the program which will forever sustain and nurture us.

GRATITUDE

"My name is George, and I'm a grateful alcoholic (addict, overeater, or gambler)!"

A statement like this might sound strange to the ears of a newcomer to a Twelve Step recovery group. How can anyone be grateful for being chemically dependent or addicted to other forms of compulsive behavior that can make our lives a living hell? Surely this is some kind of exaggeration.

Yet, when we look into the eyes of such a speaker, we can see truth there. George *is* grateful. And that gratitude seems quite astounding. (It even astounds George at times!)

What is gratitude? Where do we get it? And why is it so important? The questions are easier to ask than to answer.

Gratitude is the admission that we are not self-sufficient and don't need to be—we can get help from outside ourselves. We become grateful when we give up trying to be self-sufficient and accept help. Our very lives depend on continuing to remember what we are grateful for, and why.

Sound familiar? It should. That is the meaning of the first three Steps.

I CAN'T; GOD CAN; I'LL LET GOD DO IT!

Gratitude is the result of the Twelve Steps in action. Why is gratitude so important? For starters, it's a constant reminder that we are not alone.

Gratitude: The Antidote to Ego

Any follower of the Twelve Steps learns that the main problem we must face is living with a diseased self that is totally out of control. Bill W. wrote about this.

Selfishness—self-centeredness! That, we think, is the root of our troubles. . . . The alcoholic (user) is an extreme example of self-will run riot, though he (or she) usually doesn't think so. Above everything, we alcoholics (users) must be rid of this selfishness. We must, or it kills us! God makes that possible.

When we forget gratitude, we fall back into the trap of that diseased self. And we all do it! Self-centeredness does not die easily.

Most of us were raised to be self-reliant and independent. We weren't supposed to owe anything to anyone. We could make it on our own. In the process, we have gotten ourselves into some pretty big messes.

We are the ones who, when driving into an unfamiliar town, insist on finding our own way without stopping to ask directions. (And end up late, or lost, or both.)

We are the ones who put new pieces of equipment together without reading the instructions because we've "done this sort of thing a million times." (And it either won't work or creates a monumental mess which costs us dearly in time and money.)

We are the ones who try to direct other people's lives, even though we are totally helpless with our own. (And the consequence is usually shame and embarrassment for us and pain for them.)

Remarkably, we do all this and never notice what fools we've been. We are quite capable of making the same mistakes all over again, and very likely will. This is "self-will run riot" as Bill W. called it, and, if left untreated, can be fatal.

One of the best ways to prevent this from happening is to cultivate an attitude of gratitude. When we are grateful, we can no longer be selfish. It is a spiritual impossibility. Why? Because gratitude is the admission we are not self-reliant; it is the exact opposite of ego.

What are the earmarks of ego and self-will? False pride is one. Keeping up a good front is a constant temptation for us. Never mind that we are frightened, frustrated, and lonely at times; we do not want the world to know.

Self-pity is another symptom of ego. People seldom pay as much attention to us as we would like, and when things aren't going our way, who else can feel as sorry for us as we can? In no time at all, depression has set in and we are behind a high wall of self-pity.

Our false pride and self-pity inevitably reduce us to helplessness. We tug and pull with resentment and hostility, striving to prove our independence like defiant children. But while they cry and throw tantrums, we "grown up" children react by sulking and feeling depressed. Most assuredly we are lonely. Quite often a moment's inventory will show the problem is ego; and when we are caught up in ego, we are on our own.

The Twelve Step program teaches us to surrender. We cannot make it on our own. We couldn't when we were practicing addicts and we can't now. Bill W. reminds us that "we are not cured. . . . What we really have is a daily reprieve contingent on the maintenance of our spiritual condition." Daily contact with our Higher Power is our only hope. Gratitude is the most concrete way of acknowledging that fact.

Gratitude Is an Inventory of Assets

Sponsors often advise us to make a "gratitude list" as an antidote to the blues. The idea isn't new to us; people have been "counting their blessings" for ages. And because it is such an old-fashioned and simple idea, we might look down on it today. Experience suggests we should not.

Quite often, our moments of gloom and trouble are made more difficult by the sheer weight of problems we keep seeing in front of us. Without actually meaning to, we are doing an inventory of all the *impossibilities* that surround us, and we are defeated before we begin.

"I'd apply for the job, but I don't have enough experience to qualify me; and even though they say experience is not needed, I can't get a good recommendation from my last boss—not after the way I acted. And since I can't get a new job, I can't get shoes for the children, which means they won't be able to go to school, and then my wife will have to stay home from her job because we sure can't afford babysitters." And on and on it goes. We don't mean to be negative—far from it! It's just that our problems are so big, so visible, and so paralyzing we can't do a thing to help ourselves.

An attitude of gratitude always points us at what's going *right* for us, not what's going wrong. It may seem rather too optimistic to say, "God's in His heaven, all's right with the world," especially when some really *wrong* things are happening to us. But on the other hand, choices for action are made on the basis of possibilities, not impossibilities! I can't take a trip if all I know is the car is broken down, there's no cash for gasoline, and I can't find a map; besides, I don't know how to drive in the first place! Gratitude looks at what I *can* do. It helps me to sum up my assets and get in touch with my strengths rather than my weaknesses.

There may be many other ways to make that trip. What assets do I have? I have my health, for one. If worse comes to worse, I can walk. I have eyes and ears that work reasonably well. There's a good chance that I can follow directions. I have my wits about me and can make responsible decisions. *That's* a real blessing! And friends, let's not forget we truly are not alone. We have sponsors on whom we can rely, friends who will steady us, good people to whom we can turn for advice and help.

All these belong in our inventory of assets. And even though we are aware of problems, difficulties, and impossibilities in our lives, another source of gratitude could be these very problems that hurt so. One piece of advice that has helped me comes from the poet Noel McInnis, who wrote,

> Be loving
> of your empty times
> as well as of your full ones.
> No one has ever had a filling
> without an emptying
> to give it room.

When our friend George says, "I'm a grateful alcoholic," his words make sense, for they are a reminder that this disease the world considers such a disaster was really the making of him. He learned truth about himself, and found new faith and confidence in his Higher Power—something he very much doubts could have happened without this "disaster" called chemical dependency.

Although we certainly don't want to hang on to old character defects, sometimes our liabilities are assets in disguise. They can be valuable tools if we allow God to show us how to use them. What we need to do is cultivate positive ways of thinking and feeling to transform or replace old, negative habits.

It's hard to see how a character defect such as resentment can be an asset. It's more like a cancer that eats away our inner beings. Yet, it too can be a teacher. When Bill W. talks about making a list of our resentments, he says we must get rid of them or they'll kill us. But he also points out that they are but symptoms of a deeper disease, usually associated with our need for security or self-esteem or companionship. When resentment occurs, we can use it like a thermometer. It registers our spiritual temperature and alerts us that something is wrong. Without resentment, we would be blind to our deeper faults. With it, we can check our relationships and see how healthy they really are. We can look again at our self-image and see why we are feeling inadequate and vulnerable. We can review our relationships and test them for unhealthy dependencies, jealousy, and possessiveness. Resentment is the red flag that warns us something else is wrong. It can be very useful.

Taking an inventory of our assets puts us in touch with our strengths and enables us to act. The most painful part of personal problems is the feeling of helplessness they can create. "I'm trapped; I have nowhere to turn; there is no way out." This kind of thinking is an open door to a drink or a pill or a binge at the ice cream parlor. "I hurt so bad, I must replace my hurt with a good feeling." The trouble is, the "good" feeling is an illusion, and the "bad" feelings of guilt and failure which are sure to follow hurt even more. The helplessness is compounded and we are weaker than before.

A gratitude list looks at strengths, and points the way to possibilities instead of impossibilities. It provides us with building blocks rather than mental blocks or stumbling blocks. It is the key to action. Without a clear understanding of real possibilities, there can be no action.

Gratitude Is in the Present Tense

Practicing gratitude keeps us in the present moment. One of the most basic lessons of our program is living one day at a time. We hear this simple piece of advice more often than any other in our meetings, and for good reason. None of us can handle a lifetime of regret or remorse. It's beyond us. Countless swearings on Bibles, or on the heads of our children, or on whatever we think of as most sacred in our lives, has produced absolutely nothing. Oh, some of us learned to hang on and "white-knuckle" it, sometimes for years and years, but the experience was excruciating, and most of us found we couldn't keep it up.

Then we were told, "Do it one day at a time." This simple advice sounded idiotic at first. It was a trick of the mind, it was a mental game, and it was cheating with common sense. We knew what they *really* meant.

The real truth of the matter was we were being sold abstinence for the rest of our long, long lives.

Only this isn't playing a mind game. It is not just a trick of thinking—it is a basic fact of existence. Reality is not static; it is constantly flowing. Tomorrow becomes yesterday through the portal of today. Tonight becomes this morning through the same door. The future becomes the past in one brief moment of time—so tiny it is indivisible. The only *real* moment is *this* moment. The only time that counts is *now*. If we can deal with this moment responsibly, there is no other moment we need to concern ourselves with. The only time we can make a decision and take any action at all is *now*.

When I practice gratitude, I look at myself now. I review what has happened, and consider what may be coming, but I do it in the present tense. I learn from the past; I propose possible ways to go in the future; *I act now*.

Gratitude comes from knowing who I am, what I am, and, therefore, what I can be, with the help of my Higher Power. It protects me from the ravages of helplessness and self-pity; it reminds me of the strengths I have to meet my present moment. But best of all, it is a sure sign that I know I am not alone.

Thank God, I'm Not Alone!

Though we may not think of it this way, gratitude is an admission that we are not operating on willpower any longer. However, stubbornness persists. Self-reliance, that old habit of which we were once so proud, asserts itself. Self-will is the order of the day, and instantly we become powerless all over again. Our very refusal to reach out for help, either from our sponsor or from another friend, blocks the channel through which our Higher Power can help us. In loneliness and isolation we sicken and die. We dare not go off on our own.

I was fortunate to learn this crucial lesson early in my recovery. For several months I had sat in the back row of my meetings listening to people tell of the things God was doing for them that they could not do for themselves. I was happy for them but exempted myself. God would help them but not me: I was unworthy of God's help.

Then one evening my loneliness and self-pity grew so great I could stand myself no longer. I looked around the room, desperate for some companionship, and realized I did not know a single person in the room. I had driven forty miles from my hometown to seek the safety of total anonymity in a group in a large city. I had found it, and my anonymity was now killing me.

Then I recognized someone; I didn't know his name, but I trusted him, and reached out to grab him by the arm. "Would you sit next to me tonight?" I asked, fearful of his rejection and amazed at my own boldness. Much to my surprise, and infinite gratitude, he said, "Of course." He kept me company all through that painful meeting and took me out for coffee afterward, giving me a chance to pour out my fear and anger and frustration. He listened and understood and cared about what I was telling him. As I drove home that night, a new feeling found its way to me: hope. And it was based on the incredible notion that a total stranger had simply loved me. I found myself marveling, "If he can love me, why can't God?" The miracle of my recovery began when I found the courage to let a human being sit next to me and love me.

Since that night I have used that same path to find

God many more times. When I have lost my direction, when I am confused, angry, frightened, caught up in self-will, I seek out a friend and sit beside him. I open up my heart and let him see what's going on inside me. The result is always the same; I find my God once again.

Here is the reason for our gratitude. We are not alone. We need never be alone again. We are being helped to live our lives, one day at a time, by other people and by our Higher Power. They are doing for us what we could never do alone for ourselves.

No wonder a moment's reflection on all we have to be grateful for does us so much good. It puts us squarely in the hands of our Higher Power.

PRAYER
AND
MEDITATION

Prayer and meditation are natural processes. They are responses to our relationship with our Higher Power. That relationship has deepened throughout our individual recoveries, and for many of us this means a change in our prayer—our approach—to God as we understand God.

The prayers we once thought served our needs so well may no longer be satisfactory. Perhaps we have only used prayer as a last resort when we felt desperate or alone. As we think about our prayer life, we might see we're trying to retain old, rigid patterns of prayer which no longer reflect our present relationship with our Higher Power. Each of us has a unique relationship with God, so it is only logical to approach prayer and meditation in a more personal manner.

Some aspects of prayer, however, are common to all of us. We share the same inner need to communicate with our Higher Power. We face the same obstacles to prayer, and—although our approaches may be different—the results of our prayers can be the same: a sense

227

of closeness, a feeling of being understood, and a confidence in being heard and answered.

We may worry we are praying incorrectly, or with the wrong motives, or with poor understanding. We want to develop our conscious contact with God as we understand God, but the way to do this seems unclear.

Consequently, we find ourselves looking for the *right* way to pray, or the right place in which to pray, or the right time. We recognize the importance of our spiritual lives and see it as so important that we might fall into one of our old traps: perfectionism. This perfectionism gradually creeps into our thinking, and we tell ourselves the spirituality we desire is ours only if we perform perfectly. This booklet is not about praying the right way or about meditating in the perfect place or at a precise time. Instead, we'll look at prayer as a natural communication with our Higher Power, as part of a growing relationship.

Throughout recovery, all of our relationships have changed. Most of these, if not all, have been changes for the better. Today, we probably feel closer to our loved ones and are better able to communicate with them. The same may be true in our dealings with co-workers, casual acquaintances, or even strangers we encounter. Because we have grown, all of our relationships have also improved. This improvement is clearly evident in our relationship with our Higher Power. And in this, like our other relationships, we find we have a greater need to communicate, to talk, to share ourselves. With God, these needs find expression in prayer.

Growth in Relationships, the Twelve Step Program, and Spirituality

Our increased awareness of our Higher Power in our lives goes hand in hand with our growth in a Twelve Step program. We might have to remind ourselves to see our growth as ongoing and ever-increasing. Each time we conscientiously read and work one of the Steps, we are rewarded with more acceptance, or greater humility, or more of whatever that particular Step emphasizes. We don't constantly go back to the beginning in our program. We progress, we build, and we grow from the point where we now stand.

Our spirituality is no different. Here, too, we are constantly growing. Today we don't view our Higher Power as we did when we began a Twelve Step program, because we have shared intimate moments with God by believing God is able to restore our sanity. We have trusted God with our lives, our wills, and our innermost selves. This growth will not stop today. A week, a month, or a year from now, we will have built on today's spirituality and found an even stronger recovery and a deeper relationship with our Higher Power.

Why has this relationship with God grown so much during recovery? And why, if it has grown, do we find we desire even greater closeness? The answers to these questions for many of us exist within a Twelve Step program. The tools so essential for recovery are also the basic elements of improving our awareness of and communication with God: acceptance of powerlessness, and turning our wills and our lives over to God.

Acceptance of Powerlessness

When we accepted powerlessness, we turned toward a Power greater than ourselves. Each time we take this Step, we move closer to and have a greater need to communicate with God. When we stay in touch with the reality of being powerless—over our addictions, over other people's actions, and over the thousands of other details that bombard our lives—we are more likely to seek the serenity and comfort of prayer.

Turning Our Wills and Lives Over

Our decision here is practical as well as spiritual. It is practical because once we admit to unmanageable lives, our only hope for recovery is to turn everything over to our Higher Power. This is spiritual because we allow ourselves to accept something which is already there—the love and care of our Higher Power.

Like all relationships, no amount of love on the part of others can save us. Today, we understand what it means to love with detachment when we face addiction. Most of us have either practiced it ourselves when we realized we had no control over a loved one's addiction, or when we saw how our own family and friends finally detached themselves from our addictive behavior. In both of these instances, the act of detachment is a statement of love and of personal worth. It says, "I love you and will help you when you see you are out of control and want to help yourself." Our Higher Power has always loved and cared for us, but we finally experience this love and care when we surrender.

Almost every way we practice our program helps open us to an acknowledgment of others and a sense of our spiritual existence. We discover that we are not only mind and body, although these were probably the only two aspects of our being we focused on during our using days. Despite the joys of recovery, we may at times feel somewhat unsure of how to deal with this newly discovered or rediscovered spiritual self. We know how to stretch and develop our bodies and minds; we might not know how to exercise our spirits or even how to express them. At first, we may fall back into our old comfortable traps and try to find the "right" ways. But gradually we discover an exciting idea: how we approach our Higher Power is personal and unique, as is the way we choose to pray.

Foundations of Prayer

Our relationship with God—like our friendships—is constantly changing. Some of the principles that go into forming a friendship hold true in the development of an ongoing dialogue with God: *trust* that the friendship has potential; *pursue* the relationship; *expect* yourself to grow; *expect* something of God.

In developing all friendships and relationships, there comes that moment when we suddenly feel excited about the other person. There's a connection between us, and we sense a potential for closeness. It may not happen on the first meeting; we may even have some friends we didn't think we'd like at first. But closeness gradually develops, and we come to *trust* that the friendship has potential. This trust can be present in our prayers. It says, "I sense a closeness, and I expect this feeling to grow."

We might have already experienced some of these feelings when we felt the potential of our spirituality.

We may want to remind ourselves of the nature of spirituality: it isn't an all-or-nothing commodity; it can grow into a deeper and more beautiful partnership, especially if we believe and trust in its potential.

We've all had friendships suddenly grow stale, or we've become out of touch with a friend and the relationship withers. Our relationship with our Higher Power is no different. Contact with a friend can't be sustained in the deepest sense with a once-a-year exchange of greeting cards. Conscious contact with the God of our understanding must be *pursued*—eagerly, openly, and regularly. This doesn't mean we have to set our alarm clocks to maintain precision prayers; it only affirms the need for us to keep in touch with God if the relationship is to grow. As the theologian Helmut Thielicke said: "God is always there first, and therefore our praying is always only an answer to this simple fact."

We enter into friendships with the idea of growing. Most likely, we do *challenge* ourselves in healthy friendships. We expect ourselves to become better people—more intelligent, more caring, and more lovable. This, too, can be a part of our prayer or meditative experience.

Finally, we can *expect* something of our Higher Power. We can expect to become more fully aware of God's presence, love, and counsel. Even those of us who understand a Higher Power as being a group or as nature can expect to become aware of a great power and truth transcending that of a single person. From our earliest days in recovery, we have placed our faith in a *Power greater than ourselves*. We have experienced the reality of that Power as recovery; and now, as we consider prayer as contact with God, we can expect better understanding of God's will.

Prayer and meditation are not two distinctly different

tools for communication with our Higher Power. When we are developing a relationship, there are various ways we relate to others. Our relationships can be deepened both by active conversation and by the meaningful silences we share with those we love. We may often find our conversations lead to contemplative silences, or the thoughts that occur during silent moments suddenly need to be shared. For many of us, our relationship with our Higher Power is also expressed in both ways: the solitude of meditation, and the active communication of prayer.

Prayer

The key to any active communication is honesty. In prayer, we can honestly express our questions, doubts, fears, and even anger. Other than honesty, there is probably no restriction. A prayer can be a litany or a short outpouring of anguish. It can say, do, or be anything because it is a reflection of our needs. Prayers generally fit into several categories: guidance, praise and thanksgiving, confession, petition, and intercession.

Most of our prayers are a combination of two or more of these categories, depending on when and where they are offered. For example, we might as a daily habit pray a rambling prayer. Such a prayer may begin with wondering how we will face a particularly hard decision, recounting how we came to be in this position. From there, the prayer could be a request for guidance, a confession of wrongs we committed, and a conclusion of praise (perhaps in the sense of "Thy will be done").

We may find comfort in being able to just "talk"

with our Higher Power. This intensely personal prayer is often a sharing of thoughts, much as we do with friends. Because it doesn't exactly ask for guidance and it isn't exactly a prayer of praise, it may seem to have little specific purpose. It does have great value, however, because it emphasizes the trust and serenity of our relationship with our Higher Power.

Many of the prayers we offer in groups, in church or in a synagogue are prayers that fit into a liturgy or a set situation. For example, many of us say the Lord's Prayer at the conclusion of our meetings. A traditional table grace might be said before a meal. These prayers, although often not so personal, are beneficial because they serve as reminders of our relationship with God. If we try to think through the words, they do become more personal for us.

Meditation

Henri J. M. Nouwen, a theology professor and writer, speaks of the need for silence in his book *Out of Solitude*: "Somewhere we know that without silence words lose their meaning, that without listening speaking no longer heals, that without distance closeness cannot cure." Perhaps the balance so many of us seem to desire is so seldom found because we shun our own company. We recovering people especially may have known little joy, serenity, or calmness in the aloneness of our pasts.

The practice of meditation should hold little fear for us today. Before recovery, being alone may have meant having to face guilt, anger, and disappointments by ourselves; we probably tried to avoid ourselves, and we were alienated from a Higher Power. No wonder we feared being alone. Now we can look forward to our quiet times in which we can commune with ourselves and our Higher Power in meditation and prayer.

Meditation, like prayer, is thousands of years old and is recognized as a spiritual exercise by many of the world's major religions. Meditation allows us to shed the burdens of our physical and emotional lives by centering on simplicity. Some people relax and allow themselves the calmness of resting within the care of God. Others center on an unthreatening openness with God, uncluttered with day-to-day details. Many others have found they prefer the guided meditation of a book which gives a daily reading, message, and prayer, after which they quietly reflect on that day's reading. In any of these types of meditation, we can communicate with our Higher Power because meditation offers us an opportunity to remove our minds from the self-centered details of our lives and open our spirits to God's impressions.

How, When, and Where

Although we know there is no need to have absolute rules or guidelines for prayer and meditation, here are some suggestions which may help open us to more satisfactory communication with God.

· Trust, pursue, challenge, and expect.
· Prepare; choose a quiet place, if possible, and put everyday things out of mind.
· Listen; this can be a two-way dialogue if we're open to God.
· Surrender; we can accept once again our powerlessness.

· Discipline; we don't want to stay in touch only when
we need something. Our relationship depends on frequent contact.

While these suggestions give us a direction, they are
not absolutes. There are people who pray while driving
to work, taking an elevator, or doing the laundry. As
with any relationship, we need to feel free to say at any
time, "Oh, by the way . . ." Our need to acknowledge
God's presence and importance in our lives means we
can and may share parts of ourselves in spontaneous
prayer.

It's reassuring to know there is no right or wrong way
to pray, to know our thoughts are shared with our Higher
Power and understood, and to know there is a wisdom
and understanding which is often shared with us as we
pray.

USING
OUR
MIRACLES

ADDICTS, SOMETIME DURING RECOVERY, ALLUDE TO the "incredible coincidences" behind finding the program or facility that worked a magical abstinence and subsequent fruitful way of life. Invariably, that faith in coincidence will provoke advice from someone with more time in the program: "You are mistaken. There are no coincidences in a program combating dependencies and compulsions. What are often mistaken for magical events are really miracles for which God chooses to remain anonymous."

Those weighted down by various dependencies such as co-dependency, gambling, overeating, excessive sexual drives, or smoking, come to recognize that the miracle of surrender to reality, which starts any recovery, is not the end of miraculous experiences. They happen all the time, not to a select group, but to all who hope for spiritual progress and have faith in the program's potential for them.

When we experience miracles, we must learn to accept them as part of recovery, but must not depend on them or even anticipate them. They come to everyone in a Higher Power's time, not at mankind's bidding.

Remembering the Miracles

There can be a real danger in one's attitude toward miracles. That is the failure to recognize and *understand* the living purposes and lessons in each miracle that overwhelms us. Every miracle that happens is replete with a clear message.

Recovering addicts in hospital units and fellowships such as Alcoholics Anonymous and Narcotics Anonymous believe in miracles and accept them as part of arresting incurable addictions. That recovery has been possible for millions of Twelve Step members worldwide reminds us of the fact that miracles are still with us.

Yet, in this age of new miracles, an alarming number of those who find recovery return to their active addiction. Some regain their recovery shortly, some after more years of misery, some never. Why have they forgotten the miracles of their recovery? In practically every instance, they have failed to act. Recovering addicts cannot just see, enjoy, and forget miracles; they must apply the lesson of the miracles.

Asking for Miracles

The results of recovery's miracles are not all physical. In fact, use of any miracle is mainly emotional and spiritual. Savoring miracles through utilizing their messages brings growth and progress in all phases of living.

Forgotten miracles cease to be tools for spiritual use

when we lost sight of the fact that lifesaving events occurred because we believed they would take place. Faith and trust were added to belief. In some way, each miracle is an answer to a prayer, and this knowledge brings recovery. When belief, faith, and trust are absent, a miracle will not appear.

Miracles take substance from blind belief and childlike faith. Without frills or complications, it is easily understood, always recognizable. Such belief is nurtured by patience; God's delay in answering prayer does not mean God's denial.

The miracle makers described in the Bible and other sacred writings succeeded best (perhaps only) when there was teamwork, the recipient believing a miracle maker could and would succeed.

We benefit from our miracles only when we understand our miracles have not been outright gifts. They have been earned in some way, usually through a form of prayer. The suffering addict may merely have cried out, ''God help me'' in agony or simply held a sincere desire for recovery. Or prayer may have been a formal, on-the-knees request for help. But when it comes, the miracle is more than a blessing; it is an act of teamwork within the realm of belief. To neglect making use of such a product of wish-granting and lesson-teaching would be wasteful. We will learn from our miracles if we remember there are no demands implied in ''ask and you shall receive.''

It becomes plain that miracles are to be used for spiritual progress when one accepts a miracle as an outcome to sincere prayer. Without the recognition that prayer is behind miracles, we cannot fully understand that our *purpose in living* is in the revelations of miracles in recovery. This is more evident when, in prayer, one employs some self-examination and much meditation.

The faith within the experienced miracles should make it plain that miracles are meant to be an influence, not merely a temporary reactor. Faith is the foundation of freedom from fear. It adds security to a miracle.

Acting on Miracles

As in every other phase of a recovery program, action is the key word in using miracles. A miracle is an emotional experience and wholly positive and constructive. Even the meditative part of its magic is meant to be free of debates with oneself. Both learning and understanding, necessary elements in using the lessons of miracles, are active.

One effect of experiencing a miracle is the development of a sense of belonging in a new world—one of recovery, of love and friendship, and of caring. From this comes the desire to share, for the joys of miracles are not the sole property of the recipient. One who experiences a miracle is meant to pass its messages along. Miracles keep the dreams of recovery constant, making recovery an ongoing adventure.

The revelations of emerging from recovery miracles aren't accompanied by brilliant lights and choral music, but are the results of a growing awareness of truths. The resultant messages are practical rather than fantasy. Miracles often challenge us to refurbish and enlarge upon the elements of living that brought about the miracles—such as faith itself. One grows to trust the usefulness of a faith that can inspire a miracle. In this way, faith becomes a motivator of progress. It can change lives. After all, it inspires miracles, which are basically great changes in living patterns. For example, those who learn from living through a miracle find an attitude of doing things because they *ought to* and *want to*, rather than *must do* and *have to do*.

The changes created by miracles make clear that merely having faith is not enough to produce recovery. The recipient of a miracle cannot rest and relax. Without action, faith will fade. Unselfish, constructive action and self-sacrifice are needed to make faith effective.

A miracle creates the feeling of belonging in one who has felt its change in living. Those who have experienced the joy of a miracle need never again feel alone. To that message, a miracle adds: "Learn to care and share with others. Have faith and trust in them and you will find these assets for yourself."

Trusting in Miracles

Fear and despair disappear when a miracle takes place. Those who feel the power of a recovery miracle know anything good can and will happen, because they have seen it and accepted the change. A miracle builds both resistance to compulsions and vigilance against complacency. Furthermore, if permitted to do so, a miracle will teach that both resistance and vigilance can be natural and comfortable.

The lessons of miracles go beyond the "anything-can-happen" attitude into one that, without the taint of ego, tells the recovering addict that *what should happen* will happen. All recovering people know certain great changes have taken place because they are meant to have come true. All this is possible if the elements which produce miracles—love, gratitude, humility, honesty, faith, belief, and trust—are used to prepare addicts for really hearing at the proper time.

The belief in miracles, which made possible the sudden inspiring ability to cope with maintaining a newly discovered recovery, must not be neglected or taken for granted. Goals, once considered impossibilities by the sick mind of the addict, have materialized—and have been seen and felt. We must never forget that reality or lose the willingness to believe such miracles can take place.

With the reality of miraculous personal experiences must come vigilant awareness of reality. Our character defects never fade away completely. To think so would be an invitation to complacency and carelessness—and the approach of a slip.

The willingness to continue believing is a prime blessing of any miracle. Without an open mind and complete acceptance that a miracle is not fantasy but fact, our recovery would be much more difficult.

If there is a common denominator among those in recovery it is that we each, in some way, benefit from a personal miracle. This is what makes easy the sharing of problems and solutions. Denial makes it necessary for us to be shaken up and immersed violently into reality in order to get the idea of recovery—and miracles do this exceptionally well. After experiencing such rude awakenings, we have little trouble believing in the nearness of a Higher Power.

Growth From Miracles

An accepted miracle always brings gratitude and humility. Praying becomes more serene and tolerant, less angry and painful. We pray with a more relaxed form of courage, with fewer anxieties and less stress. Self-deception dwindles and we have a clearer vision of how to become what we want to become.

Each miracle savored will bring us closer to freedom from self-pity. Miracles expose the futility of feeling sorry for oneself and the miracle receiver learns to wipe out the tendency to wallow in self-pity. Understanding the lessons of a miracle, however, requires the ability to forgive ourselves and others. There also must be love, for without love a person cannot know how to trust.

The reality of a miracle demonstrates that, while the joy of finding a way out of suffering and into the peace of recovery is great, all pain cannot cease during change and growth. We learn from the miracle of "conversion" that pain is not ours alone. All humanity feels hurt; each person makes spiritual progress by developing trial-and-error solutions to pain. If we ignore the lessons of miracles, we face the real tragedy of never knowing the source or solution to each painful experience.

All compulsive people are excessive by nature, but our miracles show us this obsessiveness can be made useful by shifting it from overdoing harmful emotions to going to great lengths with beneficial ones. The simplest ways are learned early—listening, attending meetings, seeking new friendships, serving others. A miracle is always a positive change, never a negative one. Recovering men and women benefit most when they take time in making all changes, even the good ones.

From the realities of miracles, we can learn the vast difference between counseling others and sharing with them. The latter, with close rapport, works in areas where the advice-giving style fails.

In mutual exchange there is freedom from self-service. In a society of those who have felt miracles there are no big shots. All newcomers, flushed with their personal horror stories, quickly find their own experiences topped by those of other recovering people.

Despite the joy that overflows with every recovery miracle, each is unique and each person is happy to be allowed to march to a personal drumbeat. Miracles do not make robots of people. In fact, miracles do not happen to robots. As such, a miracle supports the idea that growth is not a measure of obeying orders but of heeding suggestions.

In the aftermath of any miracle is found the revelation that there is a great difference between serenity and complacency. Every dramatic change brings a realization that problems are solved by striving to master living problems rather than escaping from life's realities.

The honesty inherent in miracles makes it clear we cannot turn away from people, places, or things just because they bear potentials of danger to recovery. We, who have already been extremely hurt by our addiction, will not fear minor pain. Miracles show us the pleasures of coping, even if there is a modicum of pain. We, who have experienced miracles, know the foolishness of accepting the status quo. We recognize the realities of living in a modern society, backed by the support of a multitude of fellow recovering people.

A miracle is a challenge to aggressively accept the obstacles to recovery. To face the hazards of living without addictive crutches is to grow spiritually and approach true serenity. Because a miracle is not static, but often fervent action, we know the truth of the phrase, "You gotta grow or you gotta go." We know if there is no emotional growth in our recovery even serenity can become stagnated.

Although miracles do come repeatedly and bring new purposes for living with every experience, they must not become a necessity of life. Even the luckiest of recovering addicts avoid depending on a miracle to bail them out of grave situations. Miracles cannot be anticipated, but seldom fail to come to those who work the Steps patiently and diligently.

A miracle is probably the greatest evidence we will ever have that belief, faith, and trust are the most helpful gifts the mind and heart are given.

The greatest lesson brought by any miracle is that its joy must not be hoarded but passed along. When we experience a miracle of recovery we learn, above all else, that the blessings of miracles must be shared. A miracle worth cherishing is never the gift to a single person, but to countless many. With recovery miracles, it is impossible to give without receiving or receive without giving.

SERENITY

HAVE YOU EVER LOOKED AT A RECOVERING PERSON, who for many years made a career out of drinking, overeating, or caretaking, and noticed how relaxed and self-assured he or she seems to be? Perhaps you've even asked yourself, ''How can a person who before seemed so hopeless suddenly look so serene and self-confident? I wish I could look like that.''

This serene person has the God-given gift of serenity, probably a person's most powerful tool for ongoing recovery. You can achieve that state by following Step Eleven of Alcoholics Anonymous: ''We sought through prayer and meditation to improve our conscious contact with God *as we understood him*, praying only for knowledge of His will for us and the power to carry that out.'' Prayer and meditation are the keys that open the door to serenity.

What is Serenity?

Serenity is most succinctly described as a feeling of well-being. Serene people are unhurried, unharried, and unworried. They live in the here and now, not dwelling on the unhappiness of yesterday, not projecting unpleasant uncertainties into the future. Serene people are characterized by hope, love, patience, faith, humility, and honesty; praying often and enjoying feelings of self-worth and euphoria. Life for them is simple and uncomplicated.

Serene people don't get boxed in by quotas, schedules, and deadlines. They try to meet them, but they don't take the attitude that the world will come to an abrupt halt if they do not produce so much, in such and such a time. Serene people take the world as it comes. They are relaxed. They participate in sports, either as spectators or as players; they read a lot; play some musical instrument; take courses at the local school or library; do volunteer work; or visit with friends. They take ample time to engage in hobbies; go to museums, to concerts, or to the park or beach; they take long walks and observe the pleasant things. Serene people's interests are as diverse as they want them to be, and they always find time for the things they want to do.

Serenity and Resentment

Without serenity there is a fertile field for the growth of self-centeredness, resentment, depression, anxiety, despair, fear, anger, self-delusion, and withdrawal from society. Any one of these can drive a recovering person to relapse. But the two most dangerous conditions are self-centeredness and resentment.

Resentment destroys more addicts and co-dependents than anything else. Once planted, the seed grows and festers like a sore on the body. It is a constant irritant, diluting or diverting attention from more constructive or more pleasant thoughts and activities. If left unresolved, it can be ruinous.

We must learn to recognize resentments and make it a point to get rid of them, not to harbor or nurture them, lest they fester and get blown up out of proportion. By dispelling resentments, we are taking the first step on the road to achieving a serene state of mind.

Without serenity the chances are great that we may suffer from resentments and self-centeredness. And the chances are just as great that these conditions can drive us back to the bottle for physical and mental reinforcement. But worry and tension over countless problems can also hit us. Rev. Vernon Johnson categorizes these problems as legal, family, marital, financial, occupational, physical, social, and spiritual. All are potentially fatal for those who lack serenity and are not able to put them into proper perspective.

Prayer and Meditation

How, then, do we achieve serenity? Does it just come upon us all of a sudden? No way. We have to consciously work for it. We have to condition our minds to it. And the best way of doing that is through prayer and meditation.

Many people are self-conscious about praying. The macho man may relegate it to women and children, but let danger threaten him and he will inadvertently say, "God, please help me." A great many people who pray ask their God for material things, or, possibly out of fear, for forgiveness for their sins. Prayer may be either formal and prescribed, as in public worship, at the celebration of the mass, in convocation or thanksgiving; or it may be purely personal, free, and spontaneous. Public and private prayer supplement each other. But the true purpose of prayer is to establish a close relationship with a Higher Power. It need not necessarily call for falling down on our knees, clasping our hands, and bowing our heads. Most people get more out of prayer directed to a God who is standing beside them; the devout person thus enjoys a communion with God that is not possible through ritual.

Meditation? There is nothing mystical about it. It need not follow a prescribed pattern like Zen, sensory awareness, or transcendental meditation. It does not require any props or ritualistic preparation. It can be learned quickly and easily. It can be practiced on a bus, while doing the dishes or the housework, while waiting for a plane or a train in the terminal, or while waiting in line for almost anything. But the most satisfactory method of meditating is some variation of the following.

Find yourself a quiet place with subdued light. Make sure your family knows you are not to be disturbed during this time of meditation. Sit in a comfortable chair and get into a comfortable position. You may find it helps to have soft, unobtrusive music in the background. No brass. No vocals. Something like Debussy's "Afternoon of a Faun." This helps, but it is not absolutely necessary. Take a few deep breaths and exhale. Eyes closed, completely relaxed. Let your mind go blank. You will find that gradually you become wide awake inside without being aware of any particular object or idea. Keep allowing your attention to be drawn inward. Many objects and thoughts will cross your mind. Allow them to pass freely. Do not try to hold on to any one of them. If you think of a problem that is bothering you, don't try to solve it. Let it go. You will find that you become aware of being aware, of the absence of objects or ideas which can demand your attention. You will not be asleep, but you won't be aware of anything in particular. Your feelings will be euphoric. You will find yourself drifting.

Allow this state of mind to continue for ten or fifteen minutes. Do not look at your watch. It will not hurt the meditative period if you run overtime. As you progress, you will find you will rise up and become alert at the appropriate time. When you arise, you will feel like you've had a long and restful sleep. You will be invigorated and alert. You will be serene.

As time goes on, you will find you are meditating constantly. All through the day there will be brief moments when your mind will drift, when you think about nothing in particular, but pleasant thoughts pass through your subconscious. Enjoy these precious moments. They may be happening now, but you may not be aware of them until you are aware of the benefits of meditation.

Changing Our Ways

Another way to achieve serenity is to make a conscious effort to keep from being self-centered. When we think of self, we can't help but project: "What if I'm not able to pay the rent?" "What if I get sick?" "What if I lose my job?" We entertain all kinds of destructive thoughts when we think only of ourselves. It is unhealthy. Conversely, it is healthy to think of others. What are their problems and how can we help them?

We can visit them in the hospital when they are sick, take them to Twelve Step meetings; run errands for them if they are incapacitated. We can listen and sympathize when they are troubled and need a shoulder to cry on.

We can also achieve serenity by planning how we will spend our time. Going through the day without some sort of a schedule in mind is much like sailing on a rudderless ship. We keep going around in circles. One moment is just like the next. And this lack of purpose can be frustrating, bringing on a situation in which we are far from serene.

We must avoid the needless worry about performing some unpleasant task, making a difficult phone call, being friendly with a person we don't particularly like. Such things can nag us to death. If they are on our agendas, we should get them out of the way before we do anything else. This will pave the way to serenity.

Write that long-neglected letter, straighten out that jumbled closet, rearrange that messy drawer. All of these tasks are constructive and rewarding. We will think good thoughts as we do them. Our minds will be off of ourselves. We will achieve serenity. This may sound like a truism, but you will find that it does work.

Humor is also helpful in achieving serenity. We've all heard the old adage, "Laughter is the best medicine." This certainly applies in converting the blues and worries into serenity. Most of us have someone who makes us feel warm all over, who makes us laugh. This person doesn't have to be a comedian, but just someone with a sense of humor who sees something funny in almost any situation and who can transmit that lightheartedness to us. If you have such a friend, cultivate your friendship with him or her. If you don't have such a friend, seek one out; there are plenty to be found. And look for the humor in grim situations yourself.

Achieving Serenity

The Twelve Steps speak of a "spiritual awakening" as a prelude to serenity, of a personality change sufficient to bring about recovery. This spiritual awakening need not be signaled by a startling vision. Instead, the change may be gradual, hardly noticeable. Our peers may see it happening, but we may not be conscious of it. But there will come a moment when we can say, "I feel good about myself." This is our spiritual awakening, our prelude to serenity.

Once we achieve serenity, we no longer live in the past, no longer project into the future. There are no more "what ifs" or "maybes." We will live relaxed in the here and now.

After we achieve serenity, and as we go through each day, we will pray from time to time. We may say the Serenity Prayer: "God grant me the serenity to accept the things I cannot change, courage to change the things I can, and wisdom to know the difference."

Twelve Step groups have slogans like *One Day At A Time*, *Easy Does It*, *Live And Let Live*, *Turn It Over*, *Go For It*, *If It Works—Don't Fix It*, and *This Too Shall Pass*. To the uninitiated they may sound trite. But they work. By constant repetition they become part of the subconscious, and they crop up at appropriate times to remind us that all things change and we have only our recovery to concern us.

But one of our greatest freedoms is the freedom of choice. We can choose to drink or not to drink, to eat or not to eat, to be good or bad, to rescue or detach, to be happy or miserable. And if we choose to think good thoughts, we will feel good. We can, through a conscious effort, ban doubt and fear by looking on the bright side. It is just as easy to be optimistic as it is to be pessimistic. And a happy outlook will take us a long way on the road to serenity.

One word of caution. It is possible to think we have too much serenity and become careless. We can carry it to the point where we become complacent, and that can lead to relapse. Remember, we have to grow. We have to take a few calculated risks. But we must temper our serenity by contemplating small challenges and small problems we meet as we go along. There's still much to be done.

With this kind of balance, tempered with patience and tolerance, life will be more complete than we ever dreamed possible.

ABOUT THE AUTHORS

The authors of LIVING RECOVERY are men and women of all ages and from all walks of life who have had extensive experience in 12 Step living. This book is a special collection of wisdom created in the spirit of the 12 Steps and represents each writer's commitment to ''sharing what has *worked* for them.''

"EASY DOES IT BUT DO IT"
with Hazelden Recovery Books